UNTIL THERE'S
MORE TH>N
ENOUGH

UNTIL THERE'S
MORE TH>N
ENOUGH

Working Together to Transform
Foster Care Where You Live

JASON WEBER

Published in the United States of America by Credo House Publishers,
a division of Credo Communications, LLC, Grand Rapids, Michigan
credohousepublishers.com

ISBN: 978-1-62586-169-6

Cover and interior design by Frank Gutbrod
Illustrations by Lori Bailey
Editing by Elizabeth Banks

Printed in the United States of America

First edition

Contents

Not Enough?

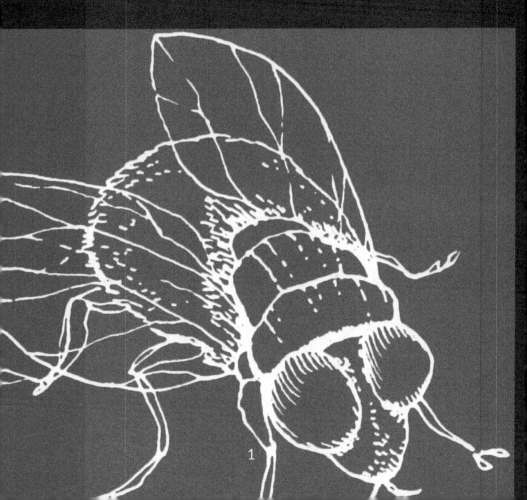

1

"We live in a world in which we need to share responsibility. It's easy to say, 'It's not my child, not my community, not my world, not my problem.' Then there are those who see the need and respond. I consider those people my heroes."

—Fred Rogers

Two of the most common words associated with foster care in the United States are **"not enough."**

- *Not enough* resources to meet all of the needs.
- *Not enough* support for struggling biological, kinship, foster, and adoptive families.
- *Not enough* families for kids who need them.

But it doesn't have to be that way where you live. There are easily enough resources, enough support, and enough families in your community to solve the foster care crisis in your county. In fact, there are more than enough.

> **Rarely do problems persist because there aren't resources to solve them. The necessary resources are almost always there. It is usually a matter of figuring out a way to route the resources that exist to the needs that persist.**

Rarely do problems persist because there aren't resources to solve them. The necessary resources are almost always there. It is usually a matter of figuring out a way to route the resources that exist to the needs that persist. The resources, support, and families that are in your community need a little help getting from where they are to the place where they are needed most.

That is where you come in.

In 2018, a team of twenty people in Germany set up over 600,000 mini dominoes in an effort to break a Guinness Book World Record. Each domino was about the size of a fingernail, and the team had spent two weeks setting them up.

And then, a single, curious, wandering fly, observing the beautiful patterns of the dominoes below, came in for a closer look. He decided to land for just a quick second to see what was going on. It is probably safe to assume that this little fella had never accomplished anything of note during his twenty-eight days of life expectancy. But, in an instant, he stumbled onto something beyond comprehension. It is something he still doesn't comprehend (both because he has a fly brain and because, well, he's dead by now). As he landed on that one domino, he set off a chain reaction that made international news.[1] A single fly rarely makes international news. He never set out to topple 600,000 dominos. His only intention was to land on one.

Maybe you were once a curious, wandering fly who, at some point, noticed the enormous number of children and families devastated by abuse, neglect, addiction, poverty, and isolation. Then one day, you decided to come in for a closer look. Maybe you volunteered to help out with at-risk kids in the community. Or you became a mentor. Or you enrolled in your first social work class. Or you took a meal over to those people from church who just became foster parents. Or you went on a mission trip. Or you showed up at an informational meeting about adoption or foster care. You landed on a domino.

The next thing you know, stuff is starting to happen. Not only are you having an impact on a child in your home or your community, but you're having an impact on several other people. Your friends are asking

> **Suddenly, you realize that God didn't just bring you into this to impact a life or two. He has a much bigger assignment in mind.**

you to dinner because they've seen what you're doing and they want to learn more. Suddenly, you realize that God didn't just bring you into this to impact a life or two. He has a much bigger assignment in mind. And then, all heaven breaks loose.

And there you are—a fly—not even beginning to comprehend the impact you're having on generations of families to come, but also the impact you're having on eternity. You thought you were just landing on a domino. You were so wrong.

While you may not have set out to do anything more than land on one domino for a closer look, you are now passionate about kids and families. And you find yourself wondering what you should do next.

That brings us to the point of this guide: What if you were able to work with the right people, on the right things, in the right way in order to transform foster care where you live? If that were to happen, I believe you could see *more than enough* become a reality for children and families in your county. By the time you get done with this book, I hope you believe it too.

This guide is a collection of insights from observing a lot of people just like you who have been seeing great results in their own counties in foster care transformation. Not only are they passionate about the children and families they fight for, they are also generous with the things they've learned. Drawing from their experiences and my own, the pages of this book reflect a set of principles and practices that can help you find allies and work together to make a bigger impact than you ever could by yourself.

It's time for the children and families in your county— to go from having ***not enough*** to having ***more than enough***. Dominos are everywhere and your job is *not* to knock them all down. Your job has only ever been to land on one. After that, you become part of something much larger, much messier, and much more magnificent than you ever dreamed.

chapter one
Painting by Number

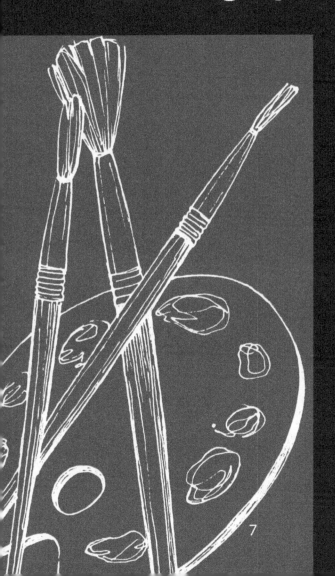

"Try to forget what objects you have before you—a tree, a house, a field, or whatever. Merely think, 'here is a little square of blue, here an oblong of pink, here a streak of yellow' and paint it just as it looks to you . . ."

—Claude Monet

"Could you paint a picture of a horse for me?"

If I asked you this and handed you a blank canvas, you would likely give me a funny look and explain to me that you are not an artist (except, of course, for those of you that are). However, if I handed you a paint-by-number of a horse and asked you to complete it, my guess is that you would be more willing. Often the difference between "I can't" and "I can" is the breaking down of something complex into manageable parts.

Leonardo Da Vinci used the paint-by-number concept as a teaching tool for his students. Dan Robbins introduced it to America as a consumer product at Macy's in the early 1950s. In fact, in 1952, someone got third place in a San Francisco art contest with a paint-by-number (likely a little embarrassing for the judges).[2]

There is no doubt that the introduction of the paint-by-number was polarizing. For example, take this quote submitted to American Artist magazine:

"I don't know what America is coming to, when thousands of people, many of them adults, are willing to be regimented into brushing paint on a jig-saw miscellany of dictated shapes and all by rote. Can't you rescue some of these souls—or should I say 'morons'?"

While some believed that the paint-by-number was the beginning of the end for our country, others disagreed. Here is another quote submitted to the same magazine:

"I know I'm not much of an artist and never will be. I've tried in vain repeatedly to draw or paint something recognizable. . .Why oh why didn't you or someone else tell me before this how much fun it is to use these wonderful 'paint by number' sets?" [3]

Love it or hate it, paint-by-number made painting accessible to everyone.

When it comes to addressing our national foster care crisis, we could learn a lot from the paint-by-number.

It is common for advocates in foster care (myself included) to cite national numbers when challenging others to respond to the needs of children in care. In fact, at the time of this writing, most people in the foster care community are familiar with numbers like "440,000" kids in U.S. foster care and "over 100,000" kids waiting to be adopted. These statistics certainly paint a picture of the enormity of the need.

However, getting time in front of a church or members of our community is a privilege. It may likely be the only ten minutes in an entire year that most of your audience is going to hear anything about foster care. To make matters worse, we use our ten minutes to talk mostly about the need for foster and adoptive parents—something that almost *everyone* listening does not feel ready to do. So when we take that traditional approach, we've made two grave errors:

1. The large numbers we use present people with a problem they know they can't solve.
2. By presenting fostering and adoption as the two primary calls to action, we provide two solutions most people don't feel they can provide.

And then, when response is low, we feel frustrated that people don't "get it" or don't "care more."

So, what if instead, we thought about foster care as an intensely local issue that every person potentially has *some* role in solving? When we advocate for kids in foster care, we need to stop sharing the biggest numbers we can find and start sharing the smallest ones. Your church leadership is *far* more willing to do something about the thirty-four kids that are waiting for adoption within twenty minutes of your church's front door than it is about the kids waiting for adoption across the country. We will succeed in addressing the foster care crisis in the United States when small, mighty bands of churches and organizations succeed in solving the foster care crisis in their own communities.

> **When we advocate for kids in foster care, we need to stop sharing the biggest numbers we can find and start sharing the smallest ones.**

Like every big problem (and every paint-by-number), we must break it down into manageable parts and take one piece at a time. Fortunately, that work has already been done for us. Today, the United States is divided into 3,142 counties or county equivalents. If a group of churches in each of those counties were to band together with each other, local organizations, and government agencies, we could truly get to *more than enough* within just a few years.

So what about your county? What would it take to get everyone going in the same direction, so that one day, your county would have *more than enough* for kids before, during, and beyond foster care? You don't have to paint the whole picture. You just need to do your part.

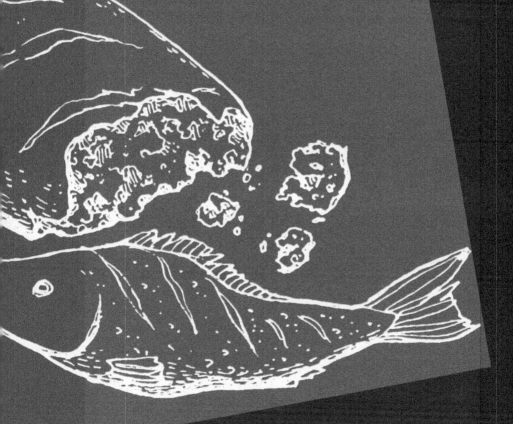

chapter two
The God of More Than Enough

"Swim down."

—Nemo

N ear the end of the Pixar movie, *Finding Nemo*, our cute little clown fish, Nemo, encounters yet another crisis when his new friend, Dory, gets swept up with hundreds of tuna fish in a giant fishing net. In a beautiful exchange, Nemo tells his dad (with whom he has just been reunited) that he knows what to do. Marlin, battling the effects of past trauma, reluctantly allows his son to spring into action. Together they instruct all the fish in the net to "swim down." The downward pressure of thousands of tuna swimming in unison begins to tear the nets that bind them. It's only a matter of moments before this giant mass of tuna (and Dory) breaks through to freedom.[4]

When it comes to big problems, real and lasting solutions require everyone heading in the same direction.

In the U.S. foster care system, most advocates in our communities and professionals in our county offices start with a clear direction: they want to see kids safe and families restored. However, over time, the nets of bureaucracy, powerlessness, overwhelming need, and limited resources cause us to feel trapped. The clear vision we once started with becomes a claustrophobic effort to simply catch a breath. We eventually settle for incremental change and hope for "just a little better." It is easy to lose sight of what it would mean to have *more than enough* families waiting for children instead of children waiting for families.

But, the truth is, we do have some small glimpses into what that looks like. In the world of adoption, it is common knowledge that there are extensive waiting lists of families waiting for healthy infants. While this is difficult and frustrating for the prospective parents who wait, when it comes to children who need families, it is precisely what we should want. Better an anxiously waiting adult than a child left to feel unwanted. Better a giant pool of parents to choose from for a perfect match than settling for the next person who answers the phone.

I pray for a day very soon when our country will be full of adults eagerly waiting for the privilege to love a nine-year-old girl for a few months, while her mom finishes up rehab; or the chance to adopt and delight in a fourteen-year-old boy with autism, who loves playing with straws; or the opportunity to mentor a seventeen-year-old who has good reason to believe that all adults are liars but is still willing to let one take him out to ice cream once a week.

> **When those in the church are willing to love hurting people, we become the embodiment of a Savior who leapt out of heaven into a dirty feeding trough to willingly expose Himself to leprosy, be ridiculed by the powerful, and endure abuse at the hands of those He came to love.**

When those in the church are willing to love hurting people, we become the embodiment of a Savior who leapt out of heaven into a dirty feeding trough to willingly expose Himself to leprosy, be ridiculed by the powerful, and endure abuse at the hands of those He came to love.

We've been commanded to love vulnerable children. So what does it look like when God's people hear one of His commands and their response exceeds expectations?

In Exodus 35, Moses delivers the message to the Israelites that God has commanded them to bring the supplies needed to build the tabernacle. This included gifts of gold, silver, and bronze, yarn and fine linen, goat hair and ram skins, acacia wood, olive oil, spices, incense, onyx stones, and other gems. Not only that, but He then commanded everyone with skill to chip in and create everything: the tent and its covering, the ark with its poles and the atonement cover, the curtain that shielded it, the table, the lampstand and lamps, the altar, the curtain for the doorway at the entrance to the tabernacle, the altar of burnt offering, the bronze basin, the curtains of the courtyard, the tent pegs for the tabernacle and their ropes, and the woven garments worn for those ministering in the sanctuary. It is a *big* list.

It was a complex and expensive undertaking, and it was all hands on deck. The passage describes the people's response to this command in beautiful detail, but it can be summed up by Exodus 35:21:

Everyone who was willing and whose heart moved them came and brought an offering to the Lord for the work on the tent of meeting, for all its service, and for the sacred garments.

Everyone brought what they could. Those with stuff brought stuff. Those with skills brought skills. And when everyone did their part, check out what happened:

They received from Moses all the offerings the Israelites had brought to carry out the work of constructing the sanctuary. And the people continued to bring freewill offerings morning after morning. So all the skilled workers who were doing all the work on the sanctuary left what they were doing and said to Moses, "The people are bringing more than enough for doing the work the Lord commanded to be done." Then Moses gave an order, and they sent this word throughout the camp: "No man or woman is to make anything else as an offering for the sanctuary." And so the people were restrained from bringing more, because what they already had was more than enough *to do all the work. (Exodus 36:3–7, emphasis added)*

> **What the people of God did here was to reflect something in God's very character: A capacity and a willingness (perhaps even a compulsion) to provide *more than enough*.**

What the people of God did here was to reflect something in God's very character: A capacity and a willingness (perhaps even a compulsion) to provide *more than enough*. We serve a God that, for whatever reason, likes to overdeliver.

When the Israelites were wandering in the desert looking for food to eat, God provided manna for them. He didn't provide "not enough." He didn't provide "just enough." He provided "*more than enough.*"

When Jesus threw an impromptu luncheon for 5,000 on the side of a hill, He didn't provide "not enough." He didn't provide "just enough." He provided "*more than enough.*"

When Jesus came across some tired fishermen who had been out all night and had caught nothing, He told them to cast their nets on the other side. He didn't provide "not enough." He didn't provide "just enough." He provided *"more than enough."*

I believe we serve a God that desires to provide for hurting children and families in this same way. I believe He wants to use us to provide them with *"more than enough."*

This begs the question, "When it comes specifically to foster care, what does '*more than enough*' look like?" We believe it applies to four areas:

- *More than enough* **foster and kinship families** for every child to have an ideal placement
- *More than enough* **adoptive families** for every child waiting for adoption
- *More than enough* help for **biological families** trying to stabilize and reunify
- *More than enough* **wraparound support** from the church for foster, kinship, adoptive and biological families

For the Christian foster care advocate, I believe that praying and fighting for **more than enough** in every one of the 3,142 counties in the country is our version of "swim down!" It will take you and the others in your community going in the same direction. It is our rallying cry, and it's time to choose **more than enough** as our destination and go there together.

Let's swim down.

chapter three
Getting from Activity to Movement

Kermit the Frog:

"Fozzie, where did you learn to drive?"

Fozzie Bear:

"Oh I took a correspondence course."

Many years ago, I was tasked with picking up a nationally known speaker at the airport in an unfamiliar city and shuttling him to a conference. This was before smartphones and GPS. The window between his landing time and his scheduled speaking time was somewhat tight, so I wanted to be well prepared. I had gone online and printed out the directions from the airport to the conference. I was ready.

However, when he got in the car at the airport, I noticed he did not have on his typical speaking attire. He asked, "Could we swing by the hotel so I can change before we head to the conference?"

I'm sure on the outside I delivered a cool and calm, "Sure, no problem."

But on the inside, I was panicking—not so much because I feared we would be late but because *I have no sense of direction*. Anyone who knows me well can confirm this. I did not think to print out maps from the airport to the hotel *and* from the hotel to the conference. I had printed *one* set of directions and now they were worthless to me.

I did manage to get us to the right zip code, and I began to feel I was recognizing things and started to feel better. At one stoplight, my passenger gently told me he thought the hotel might be the other direction from where I was about to turn (I think he had stayed there once before). But I was pretty confident at this point. I said, "I think I recognize this and am pretty sure it is this way."

Umm . . . it wasn't.

Did I mention that I have no sense of direction?

After some U-turns and some silent negative self-talk, I did manage to get my gracious passenger to his hotel and to the conference in time, but I may have shaved six months off of my life expectancy.

When I received my first GPS device as a birthday gift some years later, it was a life-changing day for me. When it came to driving, I felt like the scales had fallen from my eyes, and I could now know where I was going. Okay . . . let me rephrase that. I still didn't know where I was going, but now, I did know whether to turn right or left at the next intersection. To this day, when someone asks me where something is, I tell them that it is wherever Siri tells me it is. I'm not being cute. I am simply telling them everything I know about directions.

When I would travel to other cities, I would often find myself in the airport parking garage picking up a rental car. I'd take the GPS out of my bag and enter the address to my destination. Because the GPS device couldn't get a signal in the parking garage, the driving directions that came up would be from my home to my destination—usually a distance of hundreds of miles. In other words, my GPS knew where it was going, but it didn't know where it was. It's hard to get to where you are going if you don't know where you are. So let's talk a little bit about the beginnings of child welfare and where that leaves us today before we talk too much more about where we are going.

Charles Loring Brace, who was a minister and founder of the Children's Aid Society, saw large numbers of homeless immigrant children in New York. He began by providing for these children through various local Christian programs. Most notably, starting in 1853, he began advertising across the country for Christian families willing to take them in.[5] You will be most familiar with his work, as described by the phrase "orphan trains." As you would expect, some families welcomed children with benevolent motives, and some did so for the free labor. Over time, agencies and state governments got involved in these placements. Some states implemented the practice of paying board payments to foster families, and the idea of requiring licensure was introduced. These services became more formalized and supervised in the early 1900s.[6] The first federal agency dedicated to issues of child welfare, The U.S. Children's Bureau, was established in 1912.[7] The Social Security Act of 1935 provided the provision of federal funds for child protection.[8]

The establishment and ongoing development of the child welfare system has sought to protect hundreds of thousands of children for well over one hundred years. The standard functions and activities of the child welfare system include but are not limited to:

- Investigation of abuse and neglect allegations
- Removal of children from a home where abuse or neglect allegations are substantiated

- Provision of temporary care (foster care) for children who have been removed
- Recruitment, training, licensure, and oversight of foster families
- Oversight and implementation of case plans with the primary objective of reunifying children with their caregivers whenever possible
- Making recommendations to the court regarding next actions
- Recruitment of adoptive families for children whose parents have had their parental rights terminated by the courts
- Managing the distribution of resources to caregivers within the system

It is important to first say that each of these activities is vitally important to the well-being of children. Also, it will not come as a surprise to anyone (especially to those working in child welfare) to say that these activities are not always executed with excellence. However, without them, our children would be far worse off.

It is also worth noting that when government became involved in regulating the child welfare space, the Church backed away from it. In doing so, the Church abdicated its responsibility to care for vulnerable children and left it to the state instead.

However, over the last two decades, some new things related to child welfare have emerged from communities of faith around the country. They are grassroots, collaborative efforts that started outside of the system in the context of local churches but could not have achieved the effectiveness they have without partnership with the system. They are intensely local and comparatively inexpensive. Most importantly, they are getting incredible results. These local faith-based foster care movements are seeing the recruitment, training, and support of thousands of foster and adoptive families. They provide training and support for biological families trying to stay together and reunify, and they mobilize hundreds of volunteers to support foster care—people who never knew before that they had a vital role to play.

At its essence, a local foster care movement is made up of ...

- **families** (foster, kinship, adoptive, and biological) cared for by ...
- **churches** who are working collaboratively with each other and with ...
- **community partners** (government, placement agencies, bridge organizations, service organizations, and local businesses).

One sign that foster care movement has taken hold in a community is when a significant number of people emerge to address foster care–related needs and are not getting paid to do so. Instead of the system simply being made up of social workers, lawyers, judges, and foster families, it now includes dozens of other community members with other jobs who are "owning" the problem in their community. It's the housing contractor who offers to build a room addition for any family in his church willing to do foster care but doesn't have the space. It's the business owner who creates a space for former foster youth to learn job skills in her company. It's the homeschooling mom who teaches a single mom's child who is struggling in a traditional school environment. It's the photographer who offers free photo shoots to foster families so that a child in foster care can see a picture of themselves on the wall at home. Foster care activity often covers the the basics, but foster care movement does the rest.

In the book, *Everyone Can Do Something*, Jason Johnson writes, "This is your constant, consistent, compelling message and is reinforced every time anything is ever publicly said or written about the vision of your foster care and adoption ministry. Everyone. Can. Do. Something. Singles, college students, newly married, young families, empty nesters and retirees. Everyone."[9]

As we've already said, traditional foster care activity is incredibly important to the well-being of the most vulnerable children and families in our country. But what would it look like if we were able to go from foster care *activity* in every county in the country to foster care *movement*? What would it look like for communities to see this problem as their own and do what it takes to make the foster care crisis a thing of the past?

Before we go any further, there is a critical distinction to make here. We are talking about making the foster care *crisis* a thing of the past, *not* making *foster care* a thing of the past. Unfortunately, as long as there is brokenness in the world, there will be a need for children to be protected. In our country, the foster care system provides that. We are not trying to end foster care. However, the crisis in which our system finds itself *could* be ended in just a matter of years. There is no reason kids need to be in care for so long. There is no reason for kids to be placed in foster homes that are not good for them. There is no reason a child needs to wait for years (often in vain) for an adoptive family. There is no reason that biological families should be having to walk the journey of reunification alone. There is no reason every family associated with foster care—foster, kinship, adoptive, or biological—shouldn't have a minimum of three other families pulling for them and supporting them.

So what does it mean when we say that there is a difference between foster care activity and movement? There are five ways in which foster care activity is different than foster care movement.

1. Autonomous Action vs. Collaboration
2. Tactics vs. Vision
3. Adjustment vs. Change
4. Agency-Led Programming vs. Community-Led Advocacy
5. More vs. *More Than Enough*

The charts on the next several pages describe the difference in each of these five areas between foster care activity and foster care movement.

Foster Care Activity is . . . characterized by *autonomous action.*	Foster Care Movement is . . . characterized by *collaboration.*
Organizations and agencies (private and government) are each doing good work primarily according to their own internal quarterly and annual goals. When work is *dissimilar* between organizations, coordination of services sometimes takes place. In places where work is *similar* between organizations, competition for families, funding, government contracts, and community partnerships (i.e., churches) occurs. Because regular communication between organizations is limited, duplication of effort is common.	Organizations, agencies, and churches recognize that almost all the resources needed to solve the problem within the community already exist. It then becomes a matter of strategically figuring out who is good at what, where the holes are, and where duplication of effort can be stopped so that those resources can be redirected to fill in the gaps. This kind of collaboration cannot be accomplished without relationship. Relationship cannot be built without trust. Trust cannot be built without spending time together regularly.

Foster Care Activity is . . . driven by *tactics*.	Foster Care Movement is . . . driven by *vision*.
The most pressing visible needs generally determine programming, and those needs are addressed by tactics, including campaigns, drives, and events. The goal of those tactics is to help as many as possible (which is good). However, a compelling overall vision of a preferred future reality is missing. The result is the feeling that efforts made are merely going from one tactic to the next without a clear idea of where the plan will end up.	While strategies play an essential role, ultimately, foster care movement in a community is driven by a compelling vision toward something that is both difficult and doable. This vision provides a preferred future that everyone in the community comes to take on as their own. The visions that drive current movements are often defined by a numerical goal, geography, and a deadline. For example, "We are a group of churches working together toward *more than enough* permanent homes for forty-seven children (numerical goal) waiting for adoption in our county (geography) within two years (deadline)." Remember, tactics should always serve vision.

Foster Care Activity is . . . corrected through *adjustment.*	Foster Care Movement is . . . transformed by *change.*
Over time, the tendency to simply tweak current efforts becomes the norm. It feels very risky to try something completely different than has ever done before. What if it doesn't work? Worse yet, what if the agency gets in a huge amount of trouble for doing it? In these settings the phrase "think outside the box" is frequently used. The biggest problem with that phrase is that if one is in the box, it is very, *very* difficult to think outside of it. It's like asking a fish to describe hiking. Unless outside perspective is offered, mere adjustment is the best-case scenario, while stagnation is the worst-case scenario.	Participants in a movement recognize that achieving a preferred future requires significant change often suggested by outside perspectives. In places where movement has been successful, training schedules have been overhauled, staffing changes occur, orientation meetings have been permanently relocated, and the way services are rendered is wholly reconsidered. "We've never done it that way before" becomes a badge of honor rather than a profanity.

Foster Care Activity is ... initiated by agency-led *programming*.	Foster Care Movement is ... initiated by community-led *advocacy*.
Because agencies and organizations have put the resources into creating infrastructure, growing expertise, and developing programs, it seems only natural that they should lead the way in a community effort. The problem is that everyone else in the community will only ever feel like they are being recruited to help that agency or organization achieve its goals. It is very common for the pastor of a church to be approached by multiple such organizations in a given week addressing a variety of needs from homelessness to education to health care. Often, these organizations seem more interested in the pastor using his congregation to accomplish the organizational goals than the organization using their expertise to help the pastor achieve the congregation's vision in the community.	In this model, agencies and organizations reposition themselves from being "leaders" to being "guides." They move from being Luke Skywalker to being Yoda. Their wisdom and experiences are vital to success, but they recognize it is going to take new blood to live out the vision. They step back, set logos and egos aside, and position local churches as the leaders of the movement. Churches are *much* more likely to join with a coalition of other churches working together to transform a community than they are to sign up for a new program an agency just launched. The community wants to make itself better. Great agencies and organizations show them they can and then offer to help.

Foster Care Activity has . . . the goal of *more*.	Foster Care Movement has . . . the goal of more than *enough*.
Without a vision for a preferred future reality, the default goal simply becomes "more." We work for more resources, more families, more support. That means that we are merely trying to do better this quarter than we did last quarter. While there is nothing inherently wrong with doing "more, better, faster," it becomes a counterfeit for the real goal, which is to solve the problem.	The goal of "*more*" is traded in for the vision of "*more than enough*." This shift acknowledges what is true, but what our "realism" gave up on a long time ago: That *every* child deserves safety and permanency. It reminds the community that this is not currently true but absolutely could be. Merely getting "more" leaves children without the things they deserve. "*More than enough*" ensures that every child is cared for.

We come from a long line of a lot of amazing people who have helped countless thousands of children and families through traditional foster care activity. We should honor this immense effort and sacrifice. Even with all its faults, foster care activity has been responsible for the restoration of much brokenness. However, it's time for our communities to take this activity to the next level. We know where we've been, we know where we are, and now it's time to go where we're going.

## chapter four

More Than Enough What?

"If you don't know where you are going,
you might wind up someplace else."

—Yogi Berra

I f we want to make the transition from foster care activity to foster care movement and change our goal from "more" to "*more than enough*," it is important to define what this means. When we say that we are working toward *more than enough* in every one of the 3,142 counties or county equivalents in our country, we mean four things:

- *More than enough* foster and kinship families for every child to have an ideal placement
- *More than enough* adoptive families for every child waiting for adoption
- *More than enough* help for biological families trying to stabilize and reunify
- *More than enough* wraparound support from the Church for foster, kinship, adoptive, and biological families

Let's unpack each of those goals:

More than enough foster and kinship families for every child to have an ideal placement

In a 2017 report on the foster care housing crisis, *The Chronicle of Social Change* noted that "at least half of the states in the U.S. have seen their foster care capacity decrease between 2012 and 2017.[10] Either these states have fewer beds, and more foster youth or any increase in beds has been dwarfed by an even greater increase in foster children and youth."

A shortage of great foster homes is at the core of the foster care crisis. Great foster homes are the pivot point between the two primary outcomes of foster care: reunification and adoption. Well-trained foster parents can provide essential support, encouragement, coaching, and accountability for biological parents trying to reunify. This gives them the greatest possible chance of safely bringing their children back home. If reunification is not possible, foster parents are the most likely candidates to adopt a child that has been in their home. In fact 63 percent of children adopted from foster care in 2016 were adopted by their foster families.[11]

> **Great foster homes are the pivot point between the two primary outcomes of foster care: reunification and adoption.**

Foster care's ultimate goal is to ensure the well-being of children who have been removed from their homes. Children need more than just food and shelter, which is why we no longer rely on the orphanage model of care in this country. Children need nurture, belonging, and felt safety. Often, social workers must make placement decisions based almost entirely on one criterion: *Is there an open bed?* Because of the shortage of foster homes nationwide, this is how foster care has been operating for decades. It's not enough to aim for a "bed" for every child in care. Simply because a bed is available, does not mean it is the right environment for every child coming into care. I think we'd all agree that it would be better for kids if we could be a little pickier about their placements. The goal of having *more than enough* foster and kinship homes in a county is to allow social workers to make placement decisions that give each child the very best chance of success.

When we talk about there being *more than enough* foster and kinship families for every child to have an ideal placement, what do we mean when we say "ideal"? We have to start with the simple but profound question, *What is best for kids?* Here are critical components of an "ideal" foster care placement:

- Each child feels safe.
- Siblings stay together whenever appropriate.
- Stability is provided, thus avoiding the traumatic experience of a child moving from home to home.
- The foster parents are prepared for the child's specific age range and needs.
- The foster home is close enough to allow positive existing family and community relationships to be maintained and nurtured. Due to foster home shortfalls, children are often sent hours away from their communities. This makes it a challenge for workers to supervise a child's placement.
- The number of children in a home does not impede a child's ability to receive the care and nurturing they need.

The other vitally important way to provide safe and loving homes to children who need them is through relative placement or "kinship care." States are increasingly looking to kinship homes for temporary placement of a child. According to a 2018 article, "Forty-four states saw an increase in relative placements from 2012 to 2016."[12]

There are a few important observations to note regarding kinship families:

- Kinship families are an essential part of being able to provide *more than enough* families for children in foster care.
- Frequently they may not have otherwise considered foster parenting if a child in their family had not needed a safe place to go.
- They are often underresourced. In fact, in twenty-three of those forty-four states that saw an increase in relative placements, over half of these caregivers received no assistance.
- The number of relatives adopting children from foster care has increased by 31 percent since 2011.[13] In 2017, one-third of the 57,200 children that were adopted, were adopted by a relative.
- Kinship families are even more "hidden" in our church communities than foster families. They often need as much support (support groups, trauma-based parent training, wraparound support, etc.) as any foster or adoptive family, but may not be well connected to those resources within a church community.

Having *more than enough* great foster and kinship families in your county is going to drive success in both of the other two categories to follow. Great foster families turn into great adoptive families. Also, great foster families provide the needed support for families trying to reunify. Recruiting and keeping excellent foster and kinship families may be the most important thing we do.

More than enough adoptive families for every child waiting for adoption

When you make a phone call and are greeted with the words "your call is important to us," there are a few things you know to be true:

1. You are on hold.
2. There's a good chance the previous forty-five minutes of your day were better than your next forty-five minutes will be.
3. You are going to get the opportunity to listen to some music. It might be something you've never heard before, but there's an excellent chance it is a song called *Opus One*. (If you are curious to know why it is usually this song, you should listen to the strangely entertaining Episode 516, Act 1 of the *This American Life* podcast).

A lot of scientific effort has gone into figuring out how to make our time waiting *seem* shorter than it actually is. Hold music is one example. We know, for instance, that jazz will keep you on the phone longer than classical music. There is even a trade organization called the Experience Marketing Association (formerly called the On Hold Messaging Association) for folks that specialize in, well . . . making people wait. I decided to *not* call them for comment.

We all know that waiting is reasonable and appropriate for a lot of things. But then there are things it seems that people shouldn't have to wait extended amounts of time for. Getting a family is one of them.

It is well known that many children are waiting for adoption. But how long have they been waiting? According to the latest national available data from Kids Count:[14]

- 14 percent of children have been waiting less than twelve months
- 33 percent have been waiting between twelve and twenty-three months
- 25 percent have been waiting between twenty-four and thirty-five months
- 18 percent have been waiting between three and four years
- 10 percent have been waiting longer than five years

Time waiting: subtracting the date of a child's most recent entry into foster care from the date of the end of the fiscal year.

To summarize, 53 percent of children whose parental rights have been terminated and have a stated case goal of adoption have been waiting longer than two years in foster care.

When there are not enough adoptive families, the eventual outcome is that children age out of the system. According to ChildrensRights.org, more than 17,000 youths aged out of foster care in the United States in 2017. They noted, "Research has shown that those who leave care without being linked to forever families have a higher likelihood than youth in the general population to experience homelessness, unemployment, and incarceration as adults."[15]

People often ask, "What can we do about the problem of such large numbers of young people aging out of the foster care system each year?" And while there are some fantastic programs out there for youth that have aged out, my answer is always the same: If we want to address the problem of youth aging out of foster care at eighteen or twenty-one, then we have to do what it takes to make sure they have a loving adoptive family when they are eleven, twelve, and thirteen. When the churches in your county start providing *more than enough* adoptive homes for every child who needs one, your county will no longer have a problem with young adults aging out.

> **We all know that waiting is reasonable and appropriate for a lot of things. But then there are things it seems that people shouldn't have to wait extended amounts of time for. Getting a family is one of them.**

What would it look like to have *more than enough* adoptive families for every child who needs one in the county where you live? Well, as we've mentioned, it would look a lot like what private infant adoption looks like currently—hundreds of people waiting up to two or more years to be matched with a child. Keep in mind, this wait would not be due to system inefficiencies. Instead, it would be the result of so many people wanting to provide permanent families for older children, children with special needs, children exposed to drugs and alcohol, and children that have been abused that child welfare professionals would have the same luxury as private infant adoption workers to consider several families and make the ideal match. Even now, in some places, those seeking to adopt children under six years old are told that it may be a very long wait. That is *great*!

Yes, you read that correctly. Very soon, I *want* to see followers of Christ who would be thrilled to adopt fifteen-year-olds with autism having to wait *loooong* periods for one to become available. That is what *more than enough* looks like—waiting adults instead of waiting children. But it's okay—we're adults . . . we can take it. I've heard jazz can help.

More than enough help for biological families trying to stabilize and reunify

If you've listened to enough sermons you have undoubtedly heard this quote from 1924 Olympian Eric Liddell in the 1981 movie *Chariots of Fire*:

"God made me fast. And when I run, I feel His pleasure."[16] These are the words of a man that understood that, when it came to running, *he was made for this*.

One of the concepts in foster care that we the Church have been slow to accept is the idea of coming alongside biological families. The underlying assumption about foster care for many is that it exists to remove kids from "bad" families and put them into "good" ones.

Many people get involved in foster care to protect children. However, once you've been involved in foster care for a while, you realize that, though this is a good motivation, it is an incomplete one. Foster care at its best is also about family restoration. Perhaps some of our bias against biological families comes from the assumption that most children enter foster care because of physical or sexual abuse. However, the latest available data tells us the most common reasons children enter foster care:[17]

Neglect	62%
Parental Drug Abuse	36%
Caretaker Inability to Cope	14%
Physical Abuse	12%
Housing	10%
Child Behavior	9%
Parent Incarceration	7%
Alcohol Abuse	5%
Abandonment	5%
Sexual Abuse	4%
Child Drug Abuse	2%
Child Disability	2%
Relinquishment	1%
Parental Death	1%

All categories exceed 100 percent as more than one category can apply in each case

To be sure, the term "neglect" can be used in child welfare as a bit of a catchall. Sometimes it is applied when a child clearly needs to be removed for their safety, but suspected abuse cannot be substantiated. While some cases of neglect are severe, a parent labeled as "neglectful" is not necessarily a parent who doesn't care. Often, neglect happens due to poverty, lack of education, or addiction. While it's important not to underestimate the emotional trauma neglect can cause for a child, the behaviors that lead to neglect can be addressed. Notice that, by comparison, a relatively small percentage of children in foster care are there because of physical or sexual abuse.

When the Church began to revisit its role in taking care of vulnerable children in recent years, most people could get behind the idea of adoption and foster parenting (or at least behind the idea of other people in the church adopting and fostering). Where we have lagged behind public child welfare over the last fifteen years is this idea of restoring and reunifying families. Thankfully we are now catching up. After all, we are the ones who believe that "Therefore, if anyone is in Christ, the new creation has come: The old has gone, the new is here!" (2 Cor. 5:17). We are the ones that believe in the redemption and transformation of broken things, and we believe they can be made whole again. It is common to encounter people in the church every week who, in Christ, are overcoming addiction and brokenness of all types. We believe the God we serve is the One who "will repay you for the years the locusts have eaten" (Joel 2:25). If there's a concept that we in the Church should have been embracing all along, it's this one.

> **For far too long, we have passed off the job of restoring families in foster care to the government—a task that's nearly impossible apart from meaningful personal relationships—when we are the ones that have all the tools to do it.**

Data from 2017 suggests that 49 percent of the 247,631 children exiting foster care were reunited with their biological families. Twenty-four percent were adopted,

8 percent were emancipated, 10 percent went to live with a guardian, and 7 percent went to live with another relative.[18] That 49 percent reunification number could be significantly higher if the church were to do what it is capable of doing. No other institution has the built-in structures to facilitate reunification like the church. The Church is generally pretty good at things like addiction recovery ministry, marriage and parenting ministry, and transporting people all over the city (to visits, appointments, etc.). We have full-time paid staff in many churches dedicated to facilitating community among small groups. We have mentoring ministries, women's ministries, men's ministries, personal finance ministries, and prison ministries. For far too long, we have passed off the job of restoring families in foster care to the government—a task that's nearly impossible apart from meaningful personal relationships—when we are the ones that have all the tools to do it.

For many, the thought of interacting with biological families is scary. Most of that fear comes from never having (knowingly) met one. Certainly, the idea of building a relationship with a person who physically abuses children is daunting. As we covered earlier, that is not the story for most of the children in care. Even when it is, though we should certainly be wise, fear has no place here. As William G. T. Shedd wrote, "A ship is safe in harbor, but that's not what ships are for." As Americans, we work hard to insulate ourselves from hard things. As Christians, however, our leader modeled the opposite. He moved toward suffering and broken things. He created us to do the same.

We have all known brokenness. The God who restored each of us can restore anyone, and one of His primary tools for doing that is His people. If anyone ought to be about family restoration, it should be the family of God. Church, we were made for this.

More than enough wraparound support from the church for foster, kinship, adoptive, and biological families

Dear Liza,
There is a considerable breach in the structure of our water-carrying apparatus.
Yours truly, Henry

Dear Henry,
Well … fix it.
Respectfully, Liza

When it comes to great foster families for children, there is a hole in the bucket. According to the National Council for Adoption, "Of the estimated 200,000 licensed foster homes, between 30–60% of foster parents drop out of foster parenting each year."[19] Some of that drop-off happens for good reason. However, much of it is because we have let our foster parents down.

We have made the recruitment of new foster families a higher priority than keeping and supporting the ones we have. When you ask foster care advocates and child welfare professionals what they need, they inevitably say that we need more families. A large percentage of news articles that come across my Google alert feed about foster care note the desperate need for more families.

In a 2018 article, Jenn Rexroad noted: "Just as you would not begin filling the bathtub without first stopping the drain, the retention of resource families (foster families) should be addressed prior to or in tandem with recruitment . . . In the marketplace, no business would invest in recruiting until retention was addressed."[20]

According to a 2018 Forbes article, "it can cost five times more to attract a new customer than it does to retain an existing one."[21] Our foster care system would experience enormous transformation if we could hold on to a much higher percentage of our existing foster families. To do that, we need to better understand why they are leaving.

While parenting children from hard places can be daunting, when asked why they are leaving the system, foster parents' answers are often much more about the system itself than about a child's behavior. Many foster parents feel powerless, taken for granted, and left without adequate support. They long to be a more significant part of the decision-making process and be seen as a valued member of a child's support system rather than just a housing provider. While changing these realities within the system is vital, it's not the only way to help foster families stick it out. People are better at enduring hard things when they do not feel alone. When we as the Church church wrap around our foster families, we provide the strength they need to keep going. The best foster families are supported foster families.

Promise 686 is an organization in Georgia that trains and equips churches to wrap around families and provide the support they need. As an example, in one county where they operate, the traditional rate of retention for a foster family beyond one year is about 50 percent (this is a typical retention rate in other places as well). However, for the families being supported by their churches, the retention rate is 90 percent.

> No one should ever have to navigate something so difficult, so heartbreaking, so worthy, and so beautiful all by themselves.

As both research and observation confirm, families that are well supported are happier, more effective, and more likely to persevere.[22]

The truth is, if we rallied the troops in our churches to support foster families (something, by the way, that *a lot* more people are willing to do than become foster parents), our recruitment problem would reduce dramatically. Every foster family we retain is one foster family we don't have to recruit. This same kind of wraparound support is just as vital for our kinship, adoptive, and biological families.

The great news is that our churches are already beautifully positioned to provide this kind of wraparound support for families. We simply have to help our church members understand clearly what helps, what doesn't, and how they can get started. Most people are willing to help when there is clarity about what exactly is needed. Asking someone to generally "help out" is much less effective than asking them to babysit on Thursday morning at nine while a foster mom attends a court hearing. People want to help, they usually just don't know how. In the book, *Switch: How to Change Things When Change Is Hard,* authors Dan and Chip Heath share an incredible insight: "What looks like resistance is often a lack of clarity."[23] Yes.

More than enough wraparound support for foster, kinship, adoptive, and biological families would mean that *no one* walks through foster care alone. When said that way, it seems like it should be a nonnegotiable. No one should ever have to navigate something so difficult, so heartbreaking, so worthy, and so beautiful all by themselves.

More Than Enough: Yes, but How?

It is easy to agree that these four facets of *more than enough* are what we would all want to see become a reality in the counties where we live. However, knowing what we want and getting there are two different things. The remaining pages of this book are dedicated to providing you with the principles, strategies, and insights necessary to make *more than enough* a reality where you live. Let's start with the oldest advice first.

## chapter five

Fixing Big Stuff

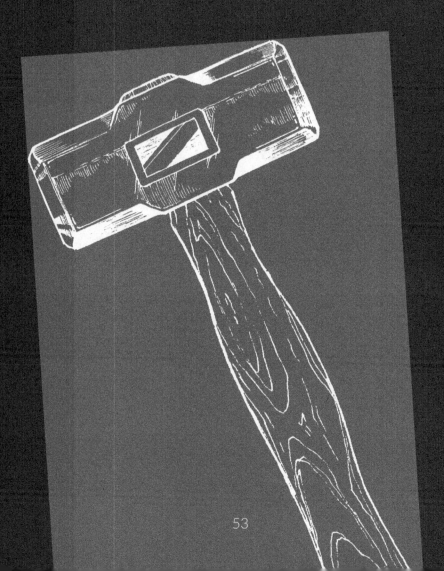

"While they were saying amongst
themselves it cannot be done,
it was done."

—Helen Keller

My wife and I have lived in and renovated a couple of different hundred-year-old-plus homes during our marriage. Most people who take on these kinds of massive projects are different from us in one important way: *They know what they are doing.*

I still remember the feeling of standing in the middle of our defunct kitchen in downtown Denver where I was hanging cabinets. I had a drill in one hand and a Black and Decker handyman book in the other trying to figure things out by looking at the hand-drawn illustrations. After all, this happened before YouTube.

> **Most people who take on these kinds of massive projects are different from us in one important way: *They know what they are doing.***

I didn't even know how to do demolition right. One night at our house in Little Rock, when Trisha and the kids were out of town, I set out to remove an old, built-in cast-iron tub (not a claw foot) from a bathroom we were turning into a laundry room. These can weigh 300-500 pounds. I always liked projects that gave me an excuse to buy a new tool, and this project was going to require a sledgehammer (sweet!). The only reasonable way to remove a tub like this is to smash it into smithereens and carry it out by the bucketful.

A little giddy, I stopped by Home Depot and selected my weapon of choice. Sledgehammer ownership is one of the true delights of human existence. I came home, put on proper eyewear, and got busy. I'm not going to lie—this is a satisfying project. Blow after blow, chunks of cast iron flew off the edges of the tub and landed on the floor.

I did overlook one small thing. On the other side of the bathroom where the toilet used to be, the water supply line was sticking up out of the floor. One of my (Thor-like) swings sent a chunk of cast iron flying across the room where its sharp edge pierced the waterline. Wetness ensued.

I wasn't sure where the shutoff valve to the house was. It would have been super smart to have located that before carrying a sledgehammer into a room full of water lines. But, alas, that's not how this went down.

Fortunately, over the years, I have had friends who knew lot more than I did about remodeling things. I was at least smart enough to know I probably shouldn't try rewiring without Steve or soldering copper pipe without Jeff. And the houses may never have been completed without David, Jason, Erin, Craig, Coletta, Adam, Mike, Brian, Doug, Joseph, and John (and a couple of youth groups some of those folks brought with them).

Big things are easier when you don't do them alone.

Maybe the best example we have of this in Scripture is found in the book of Nehemiah. After Jerusalem was destroyed (586 BC), the people of Israel were exiles in

Babylon. The Persians eventually captured Babylon, and over time, they allowed the people of Israel to return to Jerusalem in 538 and 458 BC.

In around 444 BC, Nehemiah was cupbearer to King Artaxerxes, which was a high-ranking position and a pretty good gig (except for the part where you have to test the king's refreshments for poison). Nehemiah's brother came to Susa and told Nehemiah that the wall of Jerusalem was still in shambles and that the gates that were burned had not yet been rebuilt. Nehemiah was devastated to learn this and mourned and fasted for days. King Artaxerxes saw Nehemiah's sadness and asked about it. Nehemiah told him that Jerusalem was undefended because the wall was in shambles and asked for permission to go there and rebuild the wall. Not only did he give consent, the king gave Nehemiah the ancient equivalent to an unlimited gift card to Home Depot for supplies. (Can you say, "sledgehammers"?)

Nehemiah gets his gear and organizes folks into groups and gives everyone a section of the wall to work on. Sanballat and Tobiah oppose them, forcing them to work with a tool in one hand and a weapon in the other. Even with all of that, they eventually finished the job after only fifty-two days and then celebrated in worship.

There are three specific parts of this story that are important for us to notice as we think about providing *more than enough* before, during, and beyond foster care in our communities.

1. Nehemiah believed it was possible.

When Nehemiah became aware of brokenness, he was devastated, but he believed he could do something about it. When the king asked what could be done, Nehemiah was prayed-up and was ready with an answer. He believed it was possible to fix what was broken:

> The king said to me, "What is it you want?" Then I prayed to the God of heaven, and I answered the king, "If it pleases the king and if your servant has found favor in his sight, let him send me to the city in Judah where my ancestors are buried so that I can rebuild it." (Nehemiah 2:4–5)

It's easy to take for granted that Nehemiah is the guy responsible for this, but think about how significant this was. The wall of an entire city is in shambles for decades, and this *one* guy says, "I can do something about that." He believes that it is possible.

Your community has children who have been abused and neglected and, through no fault of their own, who wait for years (often in vain) for a family. The brokenness is real. A typical response says, "That's a shame—someone ought to do something about that" (government, social workers, other "more spiritual" Christians, etc.). A Nehemiah response says, "*I* can do something about that."

2. Everyone did their part.

As you know, the Bible has many sections containing long, highly detailed lists. The temptation is to go into "skim" mode in those places. Whether it is a litany of ceremonial laws in Leviticus or a chapter on who begat whom in Matthew, it can be hard to stay with it. But when you do stay with it, every once in a while, you find gold. Or, in this particular case, gold*smiths*.

In the third chapter of Nehemiah, we get to one of my favorite snapshots in the Bible. It is simply a list of who is building what part of the wall and what they do for a living (you know . . . when they are not repairing walls). Here's a small section I especially love:

> *Uzziel son of Harhaiah, one of the goldsmiths, repaired the*
> *next section; and Hananiah, one of the perfume-makers,*
> *made repairs next to that. They restored Jerusalem as far as*
> *the Broad Wall. Rephaiah son of Hur, ruler of a half-district*
> *of Jerusalem, repaired the next section. (Nehemiah 3:8–9)*

Everyone had a part of the problem they were responsible for. Every person, regardless of occupation, had a role to play. They even let the perfumer loose on that thing. Yes . . . the perfumer.

By the way, we can also find this kind of thinking when it comes to caring for the fatherless specifically. Check out Deuteronomy 24:19–21:

> *When you are harvesting in your field and you overlook*
> *a sheaf, do not go back to get it. Leave it for the foreigner,*
> *the fatherless and the widow, so that the Lord your God*
> *may bless you in all the work of your hands. When you*
> *beat the olives from your trees, do not go over the branches*

a second time. Leave what remains for the foreigner, the
fatherless and the widow. When you harvest the grapes in
your vineyard, do not go over the vines again. Leave what
remains for the foreigner, the fatherless and the widow.

In Israel, care for marginalized people groups was woven
into the very livelihood of every person. This wasn't just
work for professional "care-ers."

> Never under-
> estimate the
ability of the perfumer
to make broken things
whole.

Are you a grain farmer? Great! Do
something to help out. Oh, you are
an olive guy or a grape lady? Doesn't
matter. You are in! Do something to
care for broken and hurting people.
Set aside a part of who you are
and what you do for the hurting, the marginalized, and the
oppressed. Everyone has a role to play.

So, what could being a project manager at a major
department store corporate headquarters possibly have to do
with transforming foster care? I know a guy who could show
you. When Keith is not at work or parenting his kids, he's
training future foster parents on the weekends for his county
as a volunteer. And he's been doing it for over a decade.

In fact, if you ask a room full of foster care advocates
from the faith community whether their educational training
or career paths have anything to do with child welfare, you
might find that very few say yes. Most people have spent
their careers doing other things. However, when needs arise,
God magically transforms these folks' gifts and skills into
loving acts of care, nurture, fierce advocacy, and resilience.

When you talk to people about foster care and think you are just there to recruit foster and adoptive families, you may very well be missing the point. There are people who may never foster or adopt, but who will transform foster care in your county in ways you could never imagine. Never underestimate the ability of the perfumer to make broken things whole.

3. They did it together.

Rebuilding the wall didn't just require everyone doing their part, they did it together. As is true with any good thing, there will be opposition. Some people don't want you to succeed; they see you as a threat:

> But when Sanballat, Tobiah, the Arabs, the Ammonites and the people of Ashdod heard that the repairs to Jerusalem's walls had gone ahead and that the gaps were being closed, they were very angry. They all plotted together to come and fight against Jerusalem and stir up trouble against it. (Nehemiah 4:7–8)

When there is a threat, it's going to take solidarity to get things done. In Chapter 4, there is a beautiful picture of this:

> Therefore I stationed some of the people behind the lowest points of the wall at the exposed places, posting them by families, with their swords, spears and bows. After I looked things over, I stood up and said to the nobles, the

officials and the rest of the people, "Don't be afraid of them. Remember the Lord, who is great and awesome, and fight for your families, your sons and your daughters, your wives and your homes. (Nehemiah 4:13–14)

The phrase I noticed here, in particular, is "by their clans." They did the work together. They defended the work together. They finished the work together.

Most followers of Christ acknowledge the theological importance of unity and the practical wisdom of collaboration. We do many things that emit the aroma of unity and collaboration. We share ideas at conferences. We get everyone together for a unifying event around an issue. We invite other organizations or churches to be a part of one of our events, and we take part in theirs. When we get together and fill up a whiteboard with brainstorming notes and nothing productive comes from it, we inoculate ourselves against wanting to collaborate in the future. We tell ourselves it isn't worth the time. However, we shouldn't give up on collaboration. Instead, we should ask whether we are engaging in the kind of interdependent unity that gets things done better than any single person, organization, or church could do by themselves.

In the book, *Rooting for Rivals,* Peter Greer and Chris Horst tell the story of several Bible translation organizations convening to figure out how they could get God's Word to people faster. Their original estimate of when the New Testament would be translated into every language was

2150. These leaders began meeting every month at the Dallas airport to discuss how they could work together to shorten this timeline. By coordinating their efforts, eliminating duplication, and focusing on areas of greatest need, the new estimate for having the New Testament in every language is now 2033. *That is a difference of 117 years!*[24]

Here's the thing about collaboration: Organizations don't collaborate, people do. You can't have meaningful collaboration without trust. You can't build trust without relationship, and you can't build relationship without spending time with someone. Gathering once a year with leaders from other organizations and churches will likely not lead to the kind of trust that is required for meaningful collaboration.

If you agree that you can't achieve *more than enough* in your county through your own efforts, then you'll need to do it with others. And to that end, you'll have to start with spending enough time talking to them on the phone and in person to build trust. If you are not interacting at least once a month with those you are collaborating with, it is unlikely that this will happen. And without that trust, meaningful collaboration leading to *more than enough* for children and families in your community will not likely be achieved.

> Here's the thing about collaboration: Organizations don't collaborate, people do.

Nehemiah has provided a great example of what it can look like to restore brokenness as a community:

1. Believe it's possible.
2. Do your part.
3. Do it together.

So, let's say you're all in. You believe it's possible. You are willing to do your part. You are committed to doing it with others. Now what? What are the essential ingredients for getting a movement launched in the community where you live? That's what we will explore next.

chapter six
Three Key Ingredients

"I bought some instant water one time but I didn't know what to add to it."

—Steven Wright

While there are many elements of building local foster care movement, three in particular are foundational: **prayer, vision, and unity.**

- Without **prayer**, a local foster care effort will be a passing fad at best, and at worst, will gain no traction at all in the hearts of the people in your community.
- Without **vision** for what could be—what should be—the status quo will prevail. And we can all agree that the status quo is letting down thousands of children and families each day.
- Without **unity**, efforts will be chaotic and contentious. Duplication of effort will be commonplace, and inefficiencies will continue to impede real progress.

You can't make chocolate chip cookies without flour, chocolate chips, or sugar (not good ones anyway). And you can't build a local foster care movement without prayer, vision, and unity. Let's take a more in-depth look at each one.

Prayer

I come from a family of hunters. Every year on the first day of pheasant season, we would wake up insanely early to go meet up with a bunch of equally sleep-deprived family friends. There's nothing quite like twenty-five sleepy people walking together through a muddy field at sunrise with loaded guns.

Decked out in three layers of clothes complete with long johns, a couple pair of socks, boots, and a stocking cap (you know—the kind with the giant pom-pom on top), I set out with these fanatically committed adults carrying my trusty BB gun.

My primary contribution to this annual excursion certainly didn't have anything to do with me shooting birds. I was valuable simply because I had feet. My job was to keep my spot in the horizontal line of people shuffling through the tall grass and stubble in the hope that my feet would scare up a pheasant that someone else with a "real" gun would shoot dead. When a pheasant emerges from the grass right in front of you crazily flapping its wings, it is a little frightening. A spare pair of long johns might have been a good idea.

Even with my BB gun, I would still take shots at things, but my hunting had little impact on the result because I did not have the needed firepower. It's hard to kill a pheasant with a BB.

Many of us march into advocacy for children with our nearly fanatical commitment, our sleep deprivation, and our strategic plan. Still, when it comes down to it, we are carrying a spiritual BB gun. We, by ourselves, are no match for the brokenness we will encounter. At its core, foster care movement is a spiritual movement, and no meaningful spiritual movement in history has started apart from prayer. That is always where spiritual movements start. As D. L. Moody once said, "Every great movement of God can be traced to a kneeling figure."

Our desired outcome for children and families impacted by the foster care system is going to require things that go way beyond what we ever could orchestrate ourselves. It will require God moving in the hearts of people to do hard things. It will require God making a way for people who disagree about a lot of things to act in unity. It will require God transforming the lives of people who are mired in generations of addiction, abuse, and mental illness. If you want to see *more than enough* happen in your community, God is going to need to show up in a big way. Prayer allows us to see firsthand His tremendous power and love in a form that can't be experienced any other way. If you've ever prayed for something big and unlikely and seen God answer that prayer, you know that it is one of the greatest privileges imaginable. If you haven't had that experience yet, get ready.

In 2007, I was part of a group of churches in Little Rock who wanted to work with local and state government to transform foster care. However, all such efforts had been met with resistance by the head of child welfare for the state. It became apparent that we weren't going to be able to go much further without something significant changing. This group of passionate foster parents, church staff, and child advocates decided to gather together for an evening to do nothing other than pray for God to open doors. We prayed specifically for this state leader and that God would make a way for our churches to help kids and families. Imagine our surprise/not surprise when several weeks later, we learned that this leader had decided to resign and move on to something else. He was replaced with an amazing woman, who could not have been more eager to partner with the church to make a difference for kids and families in foster care. That led to the birth of The CALL. Since then, CALL families have cared for over 18,000 children and created forever families for over 1,500. In fact, at the time of this writing, nearly two-thirds of all current certified non-kin foster families in the state of Arkansas were recruited and trained by The CALL. I don't know that any of us in the prayer meeting that night could have ever imagined those kinds of results. But when you ask God for something, you're going to get more than you bargained for.

> **Prayer is an expression of dependence on the only Being in existence that can get this done.**

When it comes to prayer, it's important to point out that we are *not* talking about a perfunctory acknowledgment of the existence of God at the beginning and end of our meetings. As concentration camp survivor, Corrie Ten Boom asked, "Is prayer your steering wheel or your spare tire?" Prayer is a habit of tangible admission by a group of people that we don't have what it takes to bring about the kind of change that our kids and families need.

We are utterly dependent on Him showing up. Prayer is an expression of dependence on the only Being in existence that can get this done.

When building a movement, prayer is the foundation.

Vision

One of the jobs I had in high school involved driving tractor and plowing fields to get them ready for planting. The main goal here is to drive straight. The temptation is to look just over the steering wheel to keep your front tires aligned with the previous row or to look behind you to assess your accuracy. However, the best way to plow straight is to pick something visible in the distance—an electrical pole, a fence post, or a tree—and keep your eyes fixed there.

Providing your community with a vision for foster care is just like this. It provides a tangible point of focus for everyone involved. Telling people that we must do a better job of caring for the kids and families in our community is akin to telling them to "plow straight." Yes, it is the goal, but saying it isn't that helpful. We need to pick a fence post, point it out, and invite others to go there. It will likely be some tangible expression of the overall *more than enough* vision for your county. For example:

Our vision is to see 10 percent of churches in _____ county actively engaged in foster care ministry by _____.

or

Our vision is to provide *more than enough* well-supported permanent families for all forty-eight children in _____ county waiting for adoption by

_____.

   or

Our vision is to ensure that we have *more than enough* well-supported foster families for every child in foster care in _____ county by _____.

Notice that there are numbers and timelines attached to these statements. Fence posts are solid. You know when you hit one.

On May 25, 1961, John F. Kennedy addressed Congress and made a bold proclamation, *"First, I believe that this nation should commit itself to achieving the goal, before this decade is out, of landing a man on the moon and returning him safely to the Earth."*

He didn't say it because it was popular. A Gallup poll taken after the speech revealed that 58 percent of Americans were not supportive.[25] He didn't say it because it was a virtual certainty. Many believed it was not possible. He set a vision for the United States that was hard to imagine and yet still possible. The vision was clear (land a man on the moon and return him safely) and time defined (before the decade is out).

Speaking the vision made it a priority and created focus. You have the same ability to help churches, child welfare, local businesses, and others believe that something that has never been done in your community could be a reality within a few years. It can happen, but it won't unless someone casts that vision. It might as well be you.

Unity

I don't know if you realize it, but the night before Jesus died, He prayed for you.

When I first heard this from Pastor Mark DeYmaz in Little Rock over seventeen years ago, it got my attention. John 17:20 records the beginning of this prayer: *"My prayer is not for them [the disciples] alone. I pray also for those who will believe in me through their message."*

If you believe in Jesus, you are part of this lineage. If Jesus prayed for you and me (and apparently He did), I want to know what He prayed. I mean, if I had to guess what He might pray for me hours before His death, at the top of that list would probably be obedience, faithfulness, or peace.

But He didn't. Instead, He prayed *"that all of them may be one, Father, just as you are in me and I am in you"* (John 17:21). Hours before His death, Jesus prayed that you and I would be unified.

And His prayer goes on to tell us why: *"May they also be in us so that the world may believe that you have sent me"* (John 17:21).

Unity not only makes us more effective when we are trying to solve big problems but it also helps the world believe that Jesus was, in fact, sent by the Father.

I have heard it suggested that competition between nonprofits is healthy because it spurs organizations to better, more impactful work. I've had to wrestle with what I believe about that. We all understand the place healthy competition has in business and sports, but what place, if any, does competition have in the nonprofit and church world? I do believe that when we see someone else doing good work, it inspires us to do good work. But is competition necessary for that to happen?

I don't think so. I believe that, in the arena of helping others, competition has a far greater likelihood of doing damage than doing good. The problem with welcoming competition into our work is that it necessarily begins with a misunderstanding of who our opponent is. If I am competing with you for donors, church partners, families, state contracts, or recognition, we both lose in a couple of ways. First, I am trying to get things for myself that would help you help families (and vice versa). Second, it will take each of us a lot longer to accomplish our shared objectives, which are to help as many children and families as possible. We can do that better together.

> **Unity is maybe one of the hardest things we were ever commanded to do. Sin and selfishness lobby for our autonomy. We love ourselves and our plans too much. But it is precisely because of the impossibility of unity that it shows the world that God is real and that Jesus is the one He sent.**

Don't get me wrong. Some organizations are especially good at particular things. Some models are more effective than others. So the natural process of certain programs expanding, contracting or refocusing can be positive. But that doesn't mean that we ever need to have a spirit of competition amongst ourselves, viewing resources as a tiny pie we need to fight over. Famous missionary, Hudon Taylor, once said, "God's work done in God's way will never lack God's supply."

It's the difference between seeing someone as the other team and seeing someone as a workout partner. When "they" are the other team, we think in terms of competitive advantage. We think in terms of outrunning and outscoring them. We think in terms of trying to do things better than they do them. We think in terms of winning.

But what if "they," instead, are my workout partner? That changes everything. Their success still drives me to be better, work harder, and to excel but in a completely different way. We then start thinking in terms of how to encourage each other. We think about how to get our partner to do one more set. We think in terms of both of us getting as strong as possible instead of just trying to get a little stronger than the other guy.

Not only do I think this is a more biblical way to think, I believe it's better for kids and families who are fighting generations of addiction, abuse, neglect, poverty, and hopelessness. And, by the way, if you're looking for an opponent to fight, that list of five things is a pretty decent place to start. Those are just a few of the things our real enemy is using to bring destruction to the families in your community. You want a fight? Good! Grab your workout partner and start fighting your real opponent . . . together.

Unity is maybe one of the hardest things we were ever commanded to do. Sin and selfishness lobby for our autonomy. We love ourselves and our plans too much. But it is precisely because of the impossibility of unity that it shows the world that God is real and that Jesus is the one He sent.

The Recipe for Local Foster Care Movement

No two local foster care movements look alike. Specific programs and initiatives vary, but the foundational elements remain the same. Local foster care movements are created by a group of people who are dependent on God (prayer), headed to a specific future reality (vision), and committed to doing it together (unity).

chapter seven
Getting Your Goat

"There's a way to do it better—find it."

—Thomas Edison

When my wife and I were first married, we lived in a downtown neighborhood and were part of an urban ministry. Part of our role was to help lead a high school youth ministry at a neighborhood church. One year, we set a goal to take our youth group across the country to a conference in Washington, D.C. One of the challenges was coming up with the funds to do this. In most youth groups, the leaders have the kids send out letters to family and friends to raise money for this kind of trip. However, the youth in our group did not have that kind of network, so we had to get a little creative.

We lived downtown, but I discovered when talking to my next-door neighbor one day that he owned a small ranch outside of town. He happened to mention that he had goats. I filed that little piece of intel away, and when this whole fundraising problem came up, I knocked on his door.

"Hey Pedro, you once mentioned that you had some goats out at the ranch. I was wondering if you would let us borrow one for a day?"

I'm not sure which was more unusual: The fact that I was asking to borrow a goat for a day, or the fact that Pedro didn't ask a lot of questions, but simply said, "Sure."

One Saturday morning, I drove out to the ranch, spoke briefly to one of the men working there, and loaded up a goat into the only vehicle we had available to us: our minivan. I feel like there is a fairly exclusive club of people that have had a live goat in their minivan, and I'm happy to say that I am a proud member.

We picked up the youth group kids and set off on our adventure. Pulling up to a random person's house, several teenagers (some wearing Santa hats) would pile out of our blue minivan, open the back hatch and carefully coax a goat wearing a giant red ribbon around his neck down an improvised wooden ramp onto the street. "Charlie the Christmas Goat" was on the job.

We walked up to the front door, and sometimes Charlie would leave a few initial "presents" on the sidewalk. No worries though—we had a shovel along, and as far as animal droppings go, goat droppings are relatively tidy.

We rang the doorbell, and a puzzled homeowner slowly opened the door. "Hello, we are a youth group from the neighborhood and are raising money for a trip to Washington, D.C. For a donation of any amount, we will deliver Charlie the Christmas Goat (and a Christmas carol) to anyone you wish."

Our fundraiser was a hit! People were genuinely amused to have a live Christmas goat delivering holiday cheer sent to their front door and were thrilled to send him on to friends and neighbors. One person paid us to deliver Charlie to the Mayor's house. Another sent us to a home in the suburbs that was in the middle of hosting a large Christmas party. The person at the door yelled back inside, "Hey guys, come check this out!" I think it's safe to say that

Charlie the Christmas Goat was the best thing that ever happened to a Christmas party.

They say that necessity is the mother of invention. If that is true, then foster care should be one of the most inventive systems in existence. Necessity is everywhere. It is clear that we can't get to a place we've never been using the same roads we've always used. Getting to *more than enough* in your county is going to require a great deal of innovation.

Discovering Innovation through Deeper Understanding

When I first moved to Little Rock, Arkansas, I was tasked with building relationships with local child welfare workers and administrators and finding ways to serve. My goal in these conversations with local child welfare professionals was to listen and to ask questions. It didn't take long to find out that the biggest felt need in child welfare in that community was a lack of foster families and adoptive families. They desperately needed help recruiting. I felt like we could do something about that.

I was part of a large ministry that was connected with several churches in the community. We set up a recruitment event in our sizable conference room and invited a number of area churches to come. We invited our local workers to share about the process of becoming a foster or adoptive parent. This was a first for us and we didn't know what to expect. When eighty people showed up, we thought that seemed decent. However, the county workers were absolutely thrilled. We were told at the time that it was easily the largest meeting of its type they had ever seen in the state of Arkansas.

A few weeks later, I began to get phone calls from the people that had attended the event. The reports were similar: "We've called the department and can't get anyone to call us back." Or "We signed up for a training and were told a couple days before it was supposed to start that it was canceled." My excitement about the successful event quickly faded as I realized we'd invited people to a party they couldn't get into. People were frustrated and there were clearly infrastructural and operational problems that were contributing to the shortage of foster and adoptive homes. It wasn't simply a recruitment problem. The great people at the local child welfare office weren't failing as much as they were overwhelmed and underresourced. It became clear that we were going to need to invest in helping local churches not only provide new families, but also engage with the infrastructural shortages the local offices were facing. We developed a workshop for local churches on building foster care and adoption ministry. We believed if churches had a more formal internal structure around the issue of foster care, they could then take on more systemic issues in our local child welfare system. It took some time (over a year), but our community got there. When our understanding of the problem deepened from "we need to recruit more families" to "we need to help with system infrastructure so that recruited families can get through the process," innovation resulted. Deepened understanding fuels innovation.

When these churches, led by a passionate local leader, Mary Carol Pederson, eventually started discussing how to serve our local foster care system, the infrastructural obstacles became evident. One was that orientation meetings and trainings were only held downtown, which felt a world away from the churches that were involved. At the time, state training required class attendance one evening a week for ten consecutive weeks. Conventional thinking was that if someone couldn't make a meeting for ten weeks in a row, they weren't cut out for foster care. The truth was, *great* families in churches interested in foster care were already invested in their children and their communities most nights of the week. In order to recruit and train them, something needed to change.

There was one particular meeting that included representatives from twenty-five churches, county-level workers, and state-level administrators. At one table, a formatting change to one of these training obstacles was suggested. One of the county workers at the table expressed doubt that a change like this could ever be made. At that moment, a state administrator walked by and was asked if it would be possible to make such a change. She replied, "Yes, I think we should be able to make that work."

Innovation in foster care requires three things:

1. Know *why* the old ideas are there.
2. Find new ideas that address existing gaps.
3. Make it easy for others to try new ideas.

1. Know why the old ideas are there.

We've already established that it's hard to go somewhere else if you don't know where you already are. You will come across practices in child welfare that will seem inefficient, ineffective, antiquated, and even ridiculous. Before you throw a grenade on it and replace it with something shiny and new, consider asking a couple of questions about the old practice:

- Why did we start doing it that way?
- Why have we kept doing it that way?

You might find there is a funding source that requires something to be done a certain way. Potentially this practice is the result of a grant provision or federal funding. You may also find that it is written into a contract somewhere. Remember those phone calls I got after that initial recruitment meeting about trainings getting canceled a day or two before they were to start? This was a *huge* morale killer for families who were excited to get started. We found out that this was happening because the state contract stated that the training agency could cancel a training that had less than ten people registered.

So when local church leaders went to work with county and state leaders to address the training problems, this was a vital piece of information. The churches told the state that if they were allowed to conduct foster parent training in their church buildings, they would do so without a minimum attendance requirement. The great news is that these new church-based trainings didn't struggle with a lack of registrants (in fact the opposite was often true). You can't make things better until you know why things are the way they are in the first place.

2. Find new ideas that address existing gaps.

New ideas are usually not new. They might be new to a specific county or state, but there are more and more innovative approaches emerging throughout the country in foster care. It's just a matter of finding them, studying them, and pitching them to decision-makers in your community. Here are just a few great ideas worth spreading:

- In Colorado, Project 1.27, a faith-based bridge organization, recognized that foster parents' long-term well-being and retention were correlated to the strength of each foster parent's support system. As a result, they began requiring prospective foster parents to bring at least four people from their support system to a training specifically designed for wraparound support providers like friends and extended family. The current record is held by one couple who brought twenty-eight people to the support training!

- In Michigan, one church recognized that many community members were interacting with kids from hard places—kids that church members were caring for. Unfortunately, most of the community members (teachers, counselors, coaches, medical professionals, extended family members, etc.) had not been trained to understand the unique challenges these kids were facing or how to provide support for families who were caring for them. The church set up regular events where each of their foster and adoptive families were given a round table that seats eight people. They were then invited to fill that table with any community members that had a relationship with their child. Speakers were brought in to provide trauma, behavioral, and relational training to a room full of community members who care because they have a relationship with a child.

- In Nashville, Jonah's Journey works with incarcerated mothers at the Tennessee Prison for Women. The goal of the program is to achieve reunification, if possible, by keeping mothers connected with their children. The ministry provides certified, volunteer foster families who are acting on their faith to care for both the child and the mother. This is a new way to think about foster care for a lot of churches. A program like this expands our previous understanding of foster care from "protecting children from their harmful parents" to "walking beside both child and parent in pursuit of life change."

- In several different states, Lifeline Children's Services trains churches to conduct parenting classes for families whose children have been removed by the state. The parenting class, along with others, is offered to families by the judge. The completion rate of these church-based parenting classes is significantly higher than other similar programs. This is because the church supplements the training with community, transportation, child care, and mentoring—all things that churches are uniquely equipped to provide.

This is just the tip of the iceberg. There are so many incredible Christian organizations around the country innovating amazing solutions for kids and families. Not only that, but I've found them to be some of the most generous, openhanded people I've ever met. Your best chance to innovate is to meet as many leaders doing this same kind of work around the country as you can. Use the ideas they've already tested and make new things happen in your community.

3. Make it easy for others to try new ideas.

Today's foster care system does not reward risk taking. Many working inside the system feel they have no choice but to mitigate risk at every turn. Children's lives are on the line. Legal troubles lurk within every case file. These realities can make innovation difficult. However, innovation is key to doing the best we can for kids. And it's essential if we aim to get to *more than enough*. As already mentioned, most new ideas are not new. Identifying successful programs, acknowledging the challenges encountered and overcome, and highlighting positive outcomes will lower the perceived risk to local administrators. Be thoughtful, careful, and thorough. Whether you are trying to convince a state administrator to try something new or encouraging people in your church to become foster parents, transparency is critical.

In their book *Decisive*, authors Dan Heath and Chip Heath describe a concept called "the realistic job preview." The "realistic job preview" concept is aimed at reducing employee turnover rates, which is an expensive issue in many industries. The concept was first tested in a large call center, which generally had significant turnover rates.

New applicants were shown everything that would be considered negative about the job right away. They were asked to listen to a call recording with an angry customer and were informed about the demanding hours and the hard commute. It was a bleak picture.

You would expect that being so transparent would drastically reduce the number of people who accepted the job, but it did not. The only thing it dramatically impacted was the turnover rate. The call center that employed 5,000 people saved $1.6 million due to the resulting reduction in turnover. The result of telling the unvarnished truth up front was that people felt prepared rather than surprised when difficulties arose.[26] Transparency sets accurate expectations.

My wife, Trisha, and some other local church foster care leaders were meeting monthly with the region's child welfare administrators in our county in Texas. Trisha shared early on with these administrators that we as churches were willing and ready to help, but that we were going to make mistakes. She went on to explain that the monthly meetings were meant to make sure that these inevitable mistakes got addressed quickly so that nothing would get in the way of children getting the support they needed. As promised, months later, one of our church's volunteers accidentally broke one of the protocols that had been set up. While no harm was done, it needed to be addressed. The relationship that had been established with these administrative leaders and the expectation that had been set that mistakes would occur, made it easy to own, address, and fix. It also made it easier for these government leaders to forgive the error and continue working together to help kids.

When you are pitching new ideas to others, don't shy away from exploring what could go wrong—it might be one of the wisest things you can do.

Finding New Ideas in Unexpected Places

A few years ago, our fridge went out. The meat was thawing, ice was dripping, and worst of all, the leftover ice cream cake in the freezer was in great peril. The very kind repairman told me the heater needed to be replaced. I'm no rocket scientist (or refrigerator repairman), but his diagnosis did give me pause.

I'm thinking, *My stuff is melting, and you want to install a heater in my freezer.*

He explained why refrigerators need heaters. I can't honestly say that I understood it all, but I understood enough to give the man my money so he could save my ice cream cake.

A foster care leader who's helped build church-based foster care movements in several states once shared with me that when you enter a new context—a new state, a new county, a new church—you naturally start leaping to assumptions. Your brain shouts that you need to do what makes sense based on your prior experience. But wisdom says otherwise. It tells us that when we go into a new context, our first move should be simple: just listen. As the book of James puts it, "Be quick to listen, slow to speak" (1:19). Listen to what the needs are, listen to what insiders say about the issues they are confronting.

You may not always agree. But once you've listened, you are in a much better place to help make things better. Just as important, listening well conveys the respect that is truly critical to fruitful relationships with government officials (or with anyone for that matter!)

This dynamic of jumping to conclusions about solutions can sometimes be seen when U.S. churches engage in overseas missions. We assume that the answer to poverty is money, the answer to homelessness is housing, and that the answer to lack of education is school construction. The truth is that all of these issues are incredibly complex and fraught with nuance.

I'll never forget a conversation I had with a missionary while visiting him in the country where he had worked for decades. He talked about the abandoned defunct tractors you'll find littered across the landscape. A well-meaning church or donor felt that, in the spirit of "teaching a man to fish," they would provide a tractor to encourage local agriculture. However, what they didn't anticipate is that replacement parts for that tractor are difficult or expensive to get. Mere years or even months later, this well-intentioned gift became a rather expensive piece of large yard art. If we're not careful, our ideas for problem solving in foster care can become the same thing. The real solutions to a problem may be less obvious and come from unexpected places.

Wisdom tells us that, when we go into a new context, our first move should be simple: just listen. Listen to what the needs are, listen to what insiders say about the issues they are confronting.

Be careful not to show up at that first meeting with "solutions" and too many opinions about what you think is wrong. It is extremely important that the church approach its local child welfare agency in love and humility. This first meeting is about listening and learning. The following page contains a list of questions that are designed to help prompt discussion with local child welfare professionals. Rather than serving as a script, these questions are meant to be a guide for how you might begin to engage the individual(s) that you are meeting with. They are designed to help you understand the foster care issues that affect your area and discover how churches in your community can best help address these issues.

Starting the Dialogue with Your Local Child Welfare Office

Ten questions to ask child welfare workers and administrators

1. In your opinion, what are the greatest challenges that vulnerable families in our community face?

2. What do you think would be the best course of action for helping these families so that foster care isn't a necessity?

3. What challenges have you encountered in recruiting foster and adoptive families?

4. Once a potential adoptive or foster family comes to an informational meeting, what barriers do you see that might prevent them from completing the process?

5. What new initiatives or ideas are you working on that you are most excited about?

6. In what areas of the foster care system would you most like to see change?

7. What organizations, leaders, or councils do you currently work with to coordinate efforts for community involvement?

8. Have you ever partnered with the church on the issue of foster care in the past? If so, how did it work? What were the challenges? What went well?

9. I am interested in learning as much as possible about how churches in our community can best serve kids and families in foster care. Who else should I be talking to?

10. Is there anything else you feel is important for me to know as I explore how our church and others in the community can be involved?

Increasing our impact in foster care requires laying down assumptions, listening carefully, and looking for solutions in unexpected places. Just as I learned with my freezer, the answer might be surprising . . . but it just might save your ice cream cake.

If we bring a spirit of generosity and unity to the table, things have the potential to change quickly. Let's do better at sharing innovative ideas. Let's replicate the success and innovation of others. Imagine the possibilities if we collect and share the imaginative ideas that are making a real difference across the country. Leaving a great idea to thrive in only one location is a missed opportunity. But if we listen, share, and incorporate innovative ideas that are working, all of a sudden, the idea of transforming the foster care landscape moves from passionate conversation to reality.

> **Leaving a great idea to thrive in only one location is a missed opportunity.**

Data

More Than Number

"In God we trust.

All others must bring data."

—W. Edwards Deming, Statistician

n the 1980s, the carrot industry was struggling. Not only were sales low, but waste was extremely high. Misshapen carrots did not make the cut when it came to joining their perfectly formed carrot brethren on the grocery store shelves. These unfortunate orange castaways were thrown out before ever making it to the consumer. Carrot farmer, Mike Yurosek, wanted to do something to change that. He began experimenting with turning these wasted carrots into something consumers would want. Armed with a potato peeler at first and moving on to an industrial bean cutter, he began forming large deformed carrots into cute little 2-inch carrot tubes. The rest is history.

In a Washington Times article, Roberto A. Ferdman writes:

> In 1987, the year after Yurosek's discovery, carrot consumption jumped by almost 30 percent, according to data from the USDA. By 1997, the average American was eating roughly 14 pounds of carrots per year, 117 percent more than a decade earlier. The baby carrot doubled carrot consumption.[28]

The article also states that today, "baby carrots" account for nearly 70 percent of carrot sales.[29]

Having encountered many "normal" carrots wasting away in the crisper drawer of the refrigerator prior to 1986,

I can attest that, had it not been for Mr. Yurosek's visionary leadership, my lifetime consumption of carrots would likely be nearly zero.

The simple truth is that the regular carrot is too much carrot for a regular person. It's overwhelming. It's just too much to chew.

In our desire to help people understand that we have a huge problem in foster care, we share big national numbers: there are approximately 440,000 kids in care with over 100,000 waiting to be adopted. While these are frighteningly big numbers and may be useful to a point, for most audiences they are not particularly compelling. It's just too much to chew.

People in your church would likely be *far* more motivated by the number of children in foster care in your county or even your zip code. *That* is a statistic they can do something about. Finding this kind of data is a bit more work, but worth it in terms of our ability to help people feel like their actions will make a significant difference. When you arm yourself with this kind of data, it completely changes the conversations you have with church leaders in your community.

"Pastor, sixty-two children are waiting for adoption in our county. How many of them do you feel our congregation could realistically provide homes for?"

Whatever number they give you—even if it's just one or two—multiplied by the number of churches in your community, it is very likely to be more than enough for the waiting kids in your county.

People in the nonprofit world have different feelings about data. To some, it feels too impersonal, too business-y. However, if we understand a few essential principles, we can come to realize how vital a role data plays in foster care transformation in our communities.

1. Pay attention to the ones column.

One time, when I was helping my daughter subtract large numbers for an assignment, she stacked the numbers and started on the left side in the thousands column rather than on the right side in the ones column. As you know, starting in the ones column is pretty important.

When we look at foster care data, our strong inclination is to start with the numbers on the left—the hundred-thousands and ten-thousands columns. We look for indications of trends and glimpses into the enormity of the problem we are facing.

But the first principle of handling foster care data is to pay attention to the ones column. It is the ones column that reminds us that every piece of data represents a life.

According to the most recently available national data, there were 437,283 kids in foster care on September 30, 2018. There weren't simply "over 430,000" kids in foster care on that day. There were 437,283. There are three kids in the ones column. The problem is that 400,000 is a hard number to put a name to. However, three is not.

A cursory online search of a Heart Gallery website introduces three children: Thomas, Emily, and Cameron.

When we talk about statistics, strategies, and programs, we cannot lose track of Thomas, Emily, and Cameron. I don't know them. I don't know why they are in care, what their favorite color is, or whether they like fish sticks, but I know all three of them might very well have different answers to those three questions. The way we advocate, the way we collaborate, and the way we use statistics should always be informed by the knowledge that there is a Thomas, an Emily, and a Cameron sitting right there in the ones column.

2. Data is not about sharing statistics, it is about telling stories.

Data can exist in different forms. Once it is collected, you might see it first in a spreadsheet. However, a number in a box—on a sheet full of numbers in boxes—is not very compelling. I know wonderful people who love a good spreadsheet, but let's be honest—they're not normal. A person might go the next step and pull a number from that spreadsheet and share it as a statistic. This, of course, is better—but it still leaves the audience with more questions than answers. What does that really mean? Statistics themselves can mislead, even when technically accurate. Finding the meaning behind the statistics we use is critical.

Providing context is essential. Statistics can tell incredibly compelling stories if we let them. Data-based stories are as credible as someone sharing their personal experience (i.e., I eat ice cream), but have the added benefit of being true for more than one person (i.e., 96 percent of Americans eat ice cream[30]). Take that, kale chips.

For example, I could tell you that in a given county, there were 122 children brought into foster care last year. I could go on to share that 81 of them were placed in foster homes in that county. Those are two useful statistics. But there is a critical and compelling story there, if you ask the right questions:

- If 81 of the children that were brought into foster care last year were placed within their own county, what happened to the other 41?
- Who are those 41 kids, and why weren't they placed near the things and people that are familiar to them?
- What is true of those particular 41 kids? Are they generally similar in age range, or do they have similar medical or behavioral needs?

The stats themselves don't tell you much until you hunt for the meaning behind them. In this case, the simple answer may be that there were not enough foster homes in that county. But there's a good chance it is deeper than that. You might find that most of those 41 kids required therapeutic care (a higher level of training is necessary for therapeutic foster parents). So that county might have had enough foster homes numerically, but they may not have had enough of the *right kind* of foster homes. It may be that many of those kids were medically fragile, and there weren't enough foster homes in that county equipped to care for medically fragile kids. I once heard of an instance where a little girl had some serious medical needs. Because the closest available foster home that was equipped to care for her needs was so far from a major city, she had to be life flighted to a hospital every time she needed care.

So when we talk to others about the need, that context is vital to the story we tell. Churches in your county need to know that hurting kids in their community are being sent four hours away because the necessary local families have not yet been identified and trained. As a result, those kids cannot be close to the family members, teachers, and therapists they love. That story is a lot more compelling than the fact that there were 122 kids brought into foster care last year. The stat alone is just something to be sad about, but the story the numbers tell . . . ? That story is something we must *do* something about.

3. Data provides a rallying point for collaboration.

An essential part of getting churches and organizations to work together to solve a problem is getting them to agree on what the problem is. Data paves the road toward agreement about the problem. In the county where we live, a group of ministry leaders from several churches began discussing what they could do together. After discussions with local child welfare leadership, this group eventually landed on the fact that there were sixty-two kids in the county waiting for adoption. Many of those children were older and had a variety of special needs.

This group began hosting multichurch recruitment events twice a year aimed at highlighting approximately twenty-five of the hardest to place children in the county. Each church involved sponsors a display table for one child. The church is responsible for creating a table that captures the essence of that kiddo. If that child loves horses, the table is decked out with horse stuff. If it is trucks, then that table is going to be a truck shrine. Each table at the event is then staffed with that child's caseworker and their CASA (Court Appointed Special Advocate). The child is not present. Attendees then have the opportunity to "get to know" the children in our county who have waited the longest. This group of churches has seen tremendous success in finding adoptive families for these kids. But it started with rallying around a number. Understanding the story behind the data helped these churches rally around a specific course of action that is easy to communicate to new churches.

4. Data helps you cast vision for where you are going.

When the goal in your county goes from "*more*" to "*more than enough*," the way data is used must change. When the goal is *more*, the only number you need to know is how much need there is currently. Then you just have to try to meet that need. That might lead to improvement, but it implicitly ignores the kids we are failing. However, when the goal is *more than enough*, you are demonstrating that you (and your co-collaborators) have every child in view and that you are doing all you can to meet their needs.

To do this, you are going to need some additional pieces of information. You not only need to know how many kids need care, but you also need to know how many families your county currently has. You need to know how many families you would need to exceed the demand as well. As we've already stated, it's not enough to say that if we have forty kids in care, so therefore we need at least forty-one families to get to *more than enough*. Not all of those forty-one families are equipped to care for every one of those kids. You will need to get enough available families to enable good fit–placements for older children, children with high therapeutic needs, and children that are medically fragile.

> "We need to be very comfortable with data that show us we're not having the effect we desire. Knowing what is working and knowing what is *not* working are equally valuable."
> — Nicole Wilke

While it is not an exact science, our best estimate is that approximately 2.5 certified foster families are needed for every child in care and 2.5 prospective adoptive families for every child waiting for adoption.

A word of caution here. When your county or state hears you talking about recruiting 2.5 families for every child in care, they may strongly object. After all, they don't have nearly enough resources to get that many families through the training and certification pipeline. But this should never be a reason for setting a lower goal. We can't settle for less. Admittedly, training and certification may need to be reimagined using other community resources to provide what our kids need. For example, professionally qualified members of churches have volunteered to conduct trainings or home studies. Also, part of attaining this goal is going to include the retention of existing families by supporting them well. Therefore, we won't have to recruit all new families to get to that target number—we will be keeping more of the families we already have. But we simply cannot settle for aiming at a goal that is less than what the children in our communities need.

5. Data helps you understand where you are.

It is safe to say that no one wants to waste their time on things that don't work. However, because good data outcomes can be hard to collect for local efforts, we don't exactly know whether we are as effective as we could be. Also, nonprofits can sometimes shy away from using data out of fear that it will show that they are not being effective. They rely on individual stories instead. These are powerful and effective ways to communicate with donors, but they should not be confused for evidence of effectiveness.

Nicole Wilke, the director of the Center on Applied Research for Vulnerable Children and Families, at the Christian Alliance for Orphans, shares, "We need to be very comfortable with data that show us we're not having the effect we desire. Knowing what is working and knowing what is *not* working are equally valuable." Any time we stop doing something that is not working, we make room for other things that will work. Your best chance at knowing what doesn't work is collecting good data.

6. Data gives legitimacy to your movement.

If you show up in a foreign country with a wallet full of U.S. dollars and don't bother exchanging them for the national currency, you may find your opportunities are limited. You may also end up very hungry. Two of the biggest allies in foster care transformation in your community are government and local business. These are two very different institutions, but they have one big thing in common. Their "currency" of choice is data. This is how they make decisions, how they determine priorities, and how they allot resources. If you want them to take you seriously, you will need to become comfortable handling the currency of data.

Yes, but how?

Discussions like this about data are polarizing. You are either fired up and have said "amen" three or four times over the last few pages, or you are glazed over and drooling a little on your shirt. To be transparent, I am a little closer to the drooling side of things when it comes to data. I can find it a bit overwhelming. However, I know this about myself and am intentional about collaborating with people who eat this stuff for breakfast. To lead a local foster care movement, you don't have to be a data expert, but you should know one.

> To lead a local foster care movement, you don't have to be a data expert, but you should know one.

So here is the good news for my fellow droolers: building local movement doesn't require complicated data collection. **Only collect the data you need.** Figure out what pieces of data are necessary for the specific work you are doing and collect those. Here are three questions to answer with your co-collaborators about what data you should be collecting:

1. What data matters most to our partners in government?
2. Which pieces of data are tied explicitly to our two or three most important goals?
3. Which pieces of data will be most compelling to our key audiences (churches, businesses, donors, potential families)?

How do I find foster care data that already exists?

This can be one of the more challenging aspects of local foster care movement building. Generally speaking, data that is most useful in a local movement setting is (1) up-to-date and (2) specifically local. When you do an online search for foster care data, you will likely end up with data that comes from AFCARS (Adoption and Foster Care Analysis and Reporting System). This is the system the Federal Government uses to collect foster care data from state governments. This data is then analyzed (which takes time) and released in a preliminary report containing national data about a year after it is collected. A report containing state-by-state data is released two or more years after the data is collected.[31] However, this report is not (1) up-to-date and (2) specifically local. This means that you are left presenting a problem to your community that is two to three years old and too general to be locally compelling. However, there are better options.

The best chance of finding up-to-date and specifically local data is building a trust relationship with the right people in your local or state child welfare office. They collect and use local and updated data all the time. It's just not easily accessible to the general public. However, successful agencies and organizations establish a trust relationship with the right person or department and can often get monthly county-by-county, or even zip code–by–zip code reports on foster care data. Just a warning—a simple phone call asking for foster care numbers is probably not going to yield the results you desire. Establish a relationship and be sure to help those you are building a relationship with understand your motives for seeking this data.

> **We don't just collect data to show people how great we are and to justify our existence. We collect it in order to make things better for children and families.**

To get a better idea of the information that you may want to be collecting, refer to Appendix A in the back of this book.

When Data Makes Things Better

As mentioned earlier, we shouldn't be afraid of data that shows that we are not yet achieving the results we desire. We don't just collect data to show people how great we are and to justify our existence. We collect it in order to make things better for children and families.

A 2015 *Forbes* article describes how Toms Shoes set out in 2006 to donate one pair of shoes to a child in poverty for every pair of shoes sold. This was an admirable goal to be sure. In their first year, they gave away 10,000 pairs of shoes, and in their second, 200,000.

However, what they came to understand over time was that their efforts were actually hurting local cobblers in communities around the world, disrupting local economies. Additionally, while they were putting shoes on feet, "Toms' charity didn't address the reasons why they were going without shoes in the first place."[32]

Toms used this information and pivoted. They began donating items like birth kits that include a pad, gloves, and sterile equipment to cut a baby's umbilical cord to address more systemic issues. They haven't stopped donating shoes but now attempt to source them from local shoemakers to stimulate local economies.[33]

This is an excellent example of how we can use data to learn that—despite our best intentions—we are not producing the results we intended, and then we can make a shift to do better. When we shine a bright light on a newly painted wall and reveal a thin spot in the paint, we don't go about our business feeling sad for being a lousy painter. We shine the light, find the thin spots, and fix them. Let data be your lightbulb.

chapter nine
The Actively Engaged Church

"The Church is the Church only

when it exists for others."

—Dietrich Bonhoeffer

A few years ago, as I was leaving Orlando after a conference, it became apparent upon arrival at the airport that things were backed up. The wait at the ticket counter was substantial, and security lines were long. As we all shuffled through the rope lines at security, I saw something I'd never seen before. An agent was leading a dog back and forth across the edges of the rope line. The dog was sniffing each person who walked through. When we got near the front of the line, I started hearing instructions that I was *not* used to in an airport:

"Keep your shoes *on*."

"Keep your computers *in* your bags."

It was obvious that they were trying to make things go faster, but the question going through all of our minds in line was, "Is this safe?"

The thought no sooner entered my mind than the TSA agent said this:

"When the dog is here, everything changes."

With those words, it all became clear. The simple presence of the dog made all of these other cumbersome, mechanical, time-consuming activities completely unnecessary.

This simple statement perfectly sums up what the Church can and should be in the world of child welfare.

There are churches all over the country that are having a significant impact on foster care in their communities. It's not that the Church is being heroic and saving the day. It's just that when the Church is there, everything changes. This is the Church at its best—humbly doing the job it was commanded by Jesus to do:

> *"You are the light of the world. A town built on a hill cannot be hidden. Neither do people light a lamp and put it under a bowl. Instead, they put it on its stand, and it gives light to everyone in the house. In the same way, let your light shine before others, that they may see your good deeds and glorify your Father in heaven." (Matthew 5:14–16)*

When the Church is finding families for kids, rallying around birth parents, loving on child welfare professionals, meeting needs as soon as they arise, and caring for children who have no one to care for them, it is living out its true character. It is what it was always meant to be: *the light of the world.*

More and more, we want it said in child welfare that, "When the church is here, everything changes."

Growing into an Actively Engaged Church

Organizations, agencies, and churches from across the country are working together to see more than 10 percent of the churches in every county actively engaged in foster care ministry by the end of 2025. We believe that will be enough to provide *more than enough.* The statement of this vision raises two important questions:

- Why only 10 percent of churches in every county?
- What does an "actively engaged" church look like?

Why only 10 percent of churches in every county?

The traditional narrative in faith-based foster care has been, "If every church only took care of one child, then the problem would be solved." There are a couple of problems with this statement. First, there are currently, approximately 245,014 churches in the U.S. and there are over 442,000 children in foster care on any given day (with many more than that passing through foster care in a given year). The one to one ratio is not going to get it done. Secondly, the one church for every child scenario is not what we would ideally want for children. We don't want a child cared for by a family inside of a church that may not know how to adequately love a child that has come from trauma nor know how to adequately wrap around that family. Instead, we want several families inside a church that are doing this together. Furthermore, that increases the chance that this church will grow in its ability to serve these kinds of families well.

> **When the Church is finding families for kids, rallying around birth parents, loving on child welfare professionals, meeting needs as soon as they arise, and caring for children who have no one to care for them, it is living out its true character. It is what it was always meant to be: *the light of the world.***

After a number of conversations with multiple organizational leaders and experts, the 10 percent figure was arrived upon. There are a few important things to note about that number:

- It does *not* mean that only 10 percent of churches would be *involved* in foster care. The percentage for foster care involvement would be much higher than 10 percent. What we are talking about here is 10 percent of churches being "actively engaged" in foster care. While most of this chapter is devoted to defining what that means, the simple way to state it is that these are churches where foster care is a significant part of the DNA of the church.

- It is not sufficient to simply calculate this in terms of, "How many people do we need to take in all the kids in foster care?" The reality is that by our definition of an "actively engaged" church, these churches are going to be doing *a lot* more than simply taking in kids. They are going to be involved in family reunification, driving systemic change, and community and family strengthening—all things that will reduce the numbers of children in foster care. And these are all things that really have little-to-nothing to do with foster parenting and adoption. If you put chocolate syrup in a glass of milk and stir it, it changes the look and taste of the entire glass of milk. Actively engaged churches are churches that stir things up.

What does an actively engaged church look like?

A team of leaders and advocates from churches and organizations across the country collaboratively designed and built an online church assessment to measure a church's engagement in foster care in six different areas. Each area is measured on a scale of one to ten. The following pages contain a summary of each area, as described in the assessment report:

Area 1: Recruitment

Description

Recruitment in a church is first and foremost about providing easy on-ramps for church members to get engaged in meaningful foster care–related ministry. While recruitment is often thought of in terms of courting potential foster and adoptive parents, this is only a small piece of a healthy recruiting strategy. The question to ask here is, "Have we provided a clear path in our church for everyone to do something?"

Churches with lower scores . . .	Churches with higher scores . . .
<ul><li>tend to struggle with putting opportunities for people to engage in front of their congregations.</li><li>are driven and passionate, but do not yet have clear systems in place for people to engage in family support, foster care, or adoption.</li></ul>	<ul><li>tend to be doing a good job at clearly and consistently presenting opportunities for people to care for children and support families.</li><li>have a ministry structure that includes a variety of "on-ramps" for a wide context of people in their congregation to engage with multiple levels of commitment.</li></ul>

Area 2: Communication

Description

Often, when people think of communications in a church related to foster care, they immediately think of "up-front" announcements and sermons. While these two things can be a vital part of your church's communications strategy, having healthy communications isn't dependent on these alone. Ultimately, communication is about clarity. Are there multiple things in place that make it clear to church members how they can get involved in foster care–related initiatives that your church offers?

Churches with lower scores . . .	Churches with higher scores . . .
• may still possess a strong ministry presence, but find it a challenge to prioritize the messaging of that ministry to the church as a whole. • may find it more difficult, as a result of low communication, to help unengaged people move toward more engagement.	• have a consistent communication stream about the ministries in place. This could include a strong web presence, Facebook groups, literature, announcements, and sermons in weekend service environments, etc. • present opportunities for engagement and connection clearly and broadly within the church.

Area 3: Prayer

Description

Jonathan Edwards wrote, "There is no way that Christians, in a private capacity, can do so much to promote the works of God and advance the kingdom of God as by prayer." Your goal as a church ministry should not simply be to "do a little more." Instead, your goal as a church is to be a catalyst for movement in the community where God has placed you. No spiritual movement in history has taken place apart from prayer. The children and families in your community need you and your church to be praying for them. There are structures that every church can put into place to ensure that this occurs.

Churches with lower scores . . .	Churches with higher scores . . .
• may still possess a strong ministry presence, but have yet to establish prayer as a foundational and consistent component of support. • may help families feel connected and well supported yet, at the same time, leave them spiritually underresourced.	• prioritize prayer as an essential component of the ministry, and invite the unengaged into this simple, yet important, opportunity to get involved. • help families involved in foster care, adoption, or support within their church feel cared for and covered in prayer by their church community.

Area 4: Community/Relational Support

Description

We were intended to live in vibrant community with others. While this is true for everyone, the consequences of living in isolation can be especially devastating for families who are caring for children who have experienced trauma. The church is an environment uniquely suited to provide this kind of support to those within its walls and those in the surrounding community. When a church is intentional about offering this kind of support to families, not only do they thrive, but the church experiences a richness and unity for which we were created.

Churches with lower scores . . .	Churches with higher scores . . .
• may still have many in their church that are fostering, adopting, or providing kinship care, yet without the wraparound and community support structures in place, those involved in the ministry may have the tendency to feel alone and isolated. • may have many in their church who would eagerly engage in foster care ministry, but are unclear about what, if any, structures exist to do so.	• have structures of support in place to ensure that families caring for children have the relational support they need to thrive. • may provide things like wraparound teams for families to assist with meals, babysitting, etc. • may also provide regular opportunities to connect with other families walking a similar journey so they can know that they are not alone.

Area 5: Physical/Financial Support

Description

In addition to the relational and spiritual support discussed in the previous section, financial and physical support is a critical part of a vibrant foster care ministry. Children and families have numerous tangible needs, and the church is in a unique position to provide for those needs. And they can do it with an agility that is sometimes difficult for the local foster care system, which is overburdened and underresourced. This is one of the simplest ways for anyone to get involved.

Churches with lower scores . . .	Churches with higher scores . . .
• have yet to establish ways to tangibly support families in their church and surrounding community in a structured capacity. • may leave families feeling underresourced and ill-equipped to provide the care necessary for the children they are serving. • have the opportunity to explore not only what they can do internally, but also what resources and avenues of support already exist in the surrounding community (agencies, organizations, other churches, etc.) they could potentially partner with.	• consistently provide for the physical and financial needs of foster, adoptive, kinship, and biological families. • have structures in place such as foster "closets" or adoption funds and encourage people in their church and surrounding community to contribute so that families caring for children can have the resources and supplies needed.

Area 6: Leadership

Description

One of the most important characteristics of a thriving church foster care ministry is a sustainable leadership structure. Any ministry of the church will struggle if it does not have leadership that is consistent, connected, and capable. This is particularly important in foster care ministry because most potential foster care ministry leaders are also often carrying a heavy load at home. Without structures in place to ensure continuity, keep leaders connected to church staff, and develop their leadership skills, the ministry will likely struggle to maintain, much less grow.

Churches with lower scores . . .	Churches with higher scores . . .
• will likely struggle to establish consistent programming related to foster care. • If they do have consistent programming, the leader of the ministry may likely be feeling isolated, overwhelmed, and ill-equipped to carry out their duties. • While the programming may be consistent for now, it is unlikely to be sustainable long-term.	• have leaders clearly designated for their foster care ministry. • have leaders that are consistently connected with staff or leadership of the church. • have leaders that are visible, accessible, and are actively engaged in opportunities to develop their leadership skills. • are intentional about the leadership needed for succession and expansion.

*The *More Than Enough* Church Assessment provides a simple way for multiple representatives from your church to answer questions about your church's engagement in foster care in six different areas. This free assessment takes about ten minutes and provides a full report with suggestions for next steps. To take it, go to *MoreThanEnoughTogether.org/churches/*.

A church that is actively engaged in foster care is *not* a church that has built everything it does around foster care. Rather, it is a church that thoughtfully applies its existing programs and resources to support families and children involved in foster care. This can include children's and youth ministry, mentoring ministry, recovery ministry, small group ministry, men's and women's ministry, benevolence ministry, legal advocacy ministry, music ministry, media ministry, photography ministry, and many others.

One of the most common remarks from people trying to get their church engaged in foster care is that certain church leaders don't "get it" when it comes to caring for orphans and children in foster care. The truth is that our church leaders wake up every morning and spend the best hours of their week trying to help us "get it" when it comes to evangelism, missions, purity, generosity, hospitality, discipleship, anger, and sacrificial love, etc. Yet despite their faithfulness, we don't "get it" on many of these fronts, or it takes us years to get there. Therefore, it would be wise for us to withhold judgment when our leaders don't "get" foster care like we do. Don't be mad, be present.

> The truth is that our church leaders wake up every morning and spend the best hours of their week trying to help us "get it" when it comes to evangelism, missions, purity, generosity, hospitality, discipleship, anger, and sacrificial love, etc. Yet despite their faithfulness, we don't "get it" on many of these fronts, or it takes us years to get there.

That is precisely why God has you at your church. It takes every part of the body of Christ to carry out God's purpose for our communities and our world, and this is your part.

There are three reasons you may be having trouble engaging churches in foster care:

1. You may not be talking to the right person.

Our natural first tendency when talking to a church is to go directly to the person seen to be in charge—the head pastor. Yes, churches who have pastors already passionate about foster care leading the charge can accelerate faster. However, you may find that others in a church would be better first points of contact. The difficulty with pastors is that they are faced with many decisions each week about real areas of human need. Pastors would like to be able to address all of them, but simply can't. However, if you can identify a key lay leader or member of the church staff with a particular passion for kids in foster care, you may find an ally with the bandwidth and influence to make something happen.

2. You're asking them to join your mission instead of asking how you can join theirs.

Often when organizations and agencies approach churches, they come to the church talking about things in this order:

1. There is a need.
2. We have a program to meet that need.
3. We want your people to join our program to meet the need.

Instead, we need to remember that every church leader has planted themselves in a community to make a difference in their community. They have a mission that could easily include kids in foster care. You just have to be willing to listen to their vision for their community and figure out how you can help them. So instead, the three steps might look like this:

1. What is the church's vision for its community?
2. How do children and families in crisis fit into that vision?
3. How can we use our experience to help the church accomplish its vision?

3. Directions to the on-ramps are not entirely clear.

Have you ever been driving and, due to construction or some other reason, can see the road you need to be on but simply cannot find an on-ramp to get where you know you need to go?

Foster care is very much like that for the church. The route seems encumbered by many obstacles and barriers. We, as advocates, have not always done the best job of providing straightforward and clear directions about how to get on at the right place. Often, we propose an entry point that is too lofty (adopt a fourteen-year-old) or an entry point that is too low (bring pencils for a backpack drive) that never actually leads to long-term impact.

The most helpful thing you can provide is clarity. Make the path to engagement as clear as possible.*

The Church as the Leader of Foster Care Movement in a Community

The primary difference between the way foster care has been done in your community and the way it could be done is the active engagement of the church. That easily can provide the horsepower to propel a community from *not enough* to *more than enough*. There is very little more energizing than a group of churches across denominations joining forces to make their community better. In the next chapter, we'll discuss how the church can work together with the other organizations in a community to transform foster care.

---

*For a much deeper dive into building an effective foster care ministry in your church, be sure to read *Everyone Can Do Something* by Jason Johnson. Learn More at: *everyonecandosomethingbook.com*

## chapter ten

Finding Your Ensemble Cast

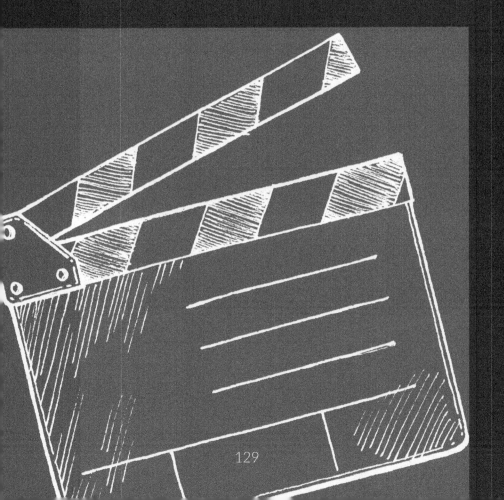

"If you want to go fast, go alone. If you want to go far, go together."

—African Proverb

A 2011 Stanford study described a collaborative approach called Collective Impact. It details five conditions for successful collaborative efforts:

1. A Common Agenda

Organizations must come to a shared understanding of the problem and an agreed-upon course of action to solve it. However, you don't have to agree on every facet of a problem. Local collaboration is not merely about working together on all our different objectives (i.e., I'll help you with aging out youth if you help me with foster family support). Instead, it is about identifying a very focused set of objectives that everyone can work toward together. There will still be things your organization works on alone—that's your role in the grand scheme of things. However, there are particular objectives that are best done together.

2. Shared Measurement Systems

My brother competes in bass tournaments in the Southwest. Teams go out in their boats and aim to catch up to five bass in the allotted amount of time. The winner is the team whose five bass add up to the highest weight collectively. Now, you can form a team and set a goal of winning a bass tournament. You can hold meetings and discuss what big bass look like and how to catch them. You can spend $150,000 on a state-of-the-art bass boat and a truck to pull it. You can attend trainings about how to catch a bass. You can catch a bunch of bass and even brag about how big they are on Facebook. But if you want to win the competition, at some point, you're going to need to put those things on an official scale. The scale in your tackle box isn't going to cut it. You have to use the scale that everyone has agreed is the official standard of success.

According to the Stanford study, "Agreement on a common agenda is illusory without agreement on the ways success will be measured and reported."[34] The goal you set needs to be measurable and how you are going to measure it should be agreed upon by everyone involved.

3. Mutually Reinforcing Activities

The most significant impact is not necessarily made by the largest number of collaborators. The key is that the actions of those involved must be differentiated and coordinated. The authors put it this way:

> Collective impact initiatives depend on a diverse group of stakeholders working together, not by requiring that all participants do the same thing, but by encouraging each participant to undertake the specific set of activities at which it excels in a way that supports and is coordinated with the actions of others.[35]

This is the body of Christ in action: the eyes doing their job while the feet do theirs. They have separate roles but work together in a coordinated and even interdependent way. When the eye sees a bear, it depends on the feet coming through to get them both out of there.

4. Continuous Communication

While seemingly obvious, the path to accomplishing this is often ignored. Trust is built between organizations over time through continuous communication. When these kinds of efforts are successful, two things are generally true: (1) the key leaders show up consistently (sending delegates to represent them hurts the effort), and (2) they connect with the other leaders as a group as often as every week but no less than once a month. If you want to be serious about transforming foster care in your community, gathering in person or by video conference at least once a month will be vital to your success.

5. Backbone Support Organization

We've already established that collaborative movement building is simply a tangible outworking of the body of Christ doing what it is supposed to do. Taking the body analogy a step further, there is a part of the body that is vital to the synthesis and coordination of all that the body does. The backbone protects the spinal cord, which synthesizes and coordinates the activity of all the parts of the body. It provides structure and establishes the posture of the entire body. It recognizes its role and clearly understands that while it has a coordinating presence, it is not the head, and does not carry itself as such.

According to Kania and Kramer:

The expectation that collaboration can occur without a supporting infrastructure is one of the most frequent reasons why it fails.

The backbone organization requires a dedicated staff separate from the participating organizations who can plan, manage, and support the initiative through ongoing facilitation, technology and communications support, data collection and reporting, and handling the myriad logistical and administrative details needed for the initiative to function smoothly.[36]

In a local foster care movement, there will be one organization that plays this role. It will not be able to do so effectively if it has not earned the trust of the others involved. In the coming descriptions of the different types of community partners, it has most often been the bridge organization (though not always) that has both the bandwidth and the trust to carry out this role. Both trust and bandwidth are vital.

Your Ensemble Cast

I have always loved TV shows and movies with an ensemble cast. As a teenager, I watched shows like *WKRP in Cincinnati, Mash,* and *Taxi.* And I have always loved movies like *Ocean's Eleven, The Lord of the Rings,* and *Guardians of the Galaxy.* I enjoy watching a group of quirky characters all in the same space trying to get something done. Don't get me wrong—hero stories that center around one main character are great, but it's the movies with the ensemble cast that always intrigued me. My favorite one might just be *The Muppet Movie*.

With an ensemble cast, you get a lot of different personalities. You get to see them when they struggle and when they shine. Consider just a few of the Muppets, for example:

Character	When They Struggle	When They Shine
Kermit the Frog	Insecure, melancholy, fearful	A kind, visionary leader who gathers and inspires the best in others
Fozzy Bear	Starved for the approval of others, lacks self-awareness	Resilient (his jokes consistently bomb on stage, and he never gives up), loyal
Miss Piggy	Narcissistic, short-tempered, competitive, overbearing	Strong, confident
The Great Gonzo	Socially inappropriate, unpredictable	Fearless, enthusiastic, strong sense of self, soulful
Animal	Destroys everything	Destroys everything (and sometimes saves the day doing it)

Here's a recap of the movie: Kermit the Frog has a dream of going to Hollywood to become a star. As he sets out from his lily pad–filled swamp to go across the country on his journey, he picks up fellow dreamers along the way. Kermit doesn't get the luxury of picking out exactly who he wants to come along. He just gathers those that have a dream similar to his.[37] With all of their gifts *and* their faults, they start heading toward the dream together.

This is the exact scenario you will find yourself in when it comes to achieving *more than enough* in the community where you live. You don't get to pick the cast. They are already there. It consists of government agencies, private agencies, organizations, businesses, and churches in your community. You'll see them at their best and their worst. However, you will get the privilege of sharing a common vision and going there together.

Earlier, we mentioned that, at its essence, a local foster care movement is about . . .

- **families** (foster, kinship, adoptive, and biological) cared for by . . .
- **churches** who are working collaboratively with each other, and with . . .
- **community partners.**

A thriving foster care movement may have as many as five different kinds of community partners supporting a group of churches to transform foster care in their community:

1. Government
2. Private child placement agencies (CPAs)
3. Bridge organizations
4. Service organizations
5. Local businesses

This local network of churches and their community partners is your ensemble cast. Let's provide an overview description of each.

1. Government

Government is responsible for child protection through the foster care system. According to the Children's Bureau, the government oversees four main facets of child welfare:[38]

- "Receive and investigate reports of possible child abuse and neglect"
- "Provide services to families that need assistance in the protection and care of their children"
- "Arrange for children to live with kin or with foster families when they are not safe at home"
- "Arrange for reunification, adoption, or other permanent family connections for children leaving foster care"

These systems can be state-administered (managed primarily at the state level), county-administered (managed primarily at the county level), or a hybrid between the two. Regardless of how it is administered, the system is subject to both state and federal law. The majority of states have state-administered systems.

As Christians, we believe God has delegated to government a critical role in ensuring justice (for example, see Romans 13:3–4). That means protecting the innocent from harm, including children, and punishing perpetrators. A well-run child protection system is a key expression of this God-given role. Because the government legally has custody of the children in its care, partnership with government agencies is necessary to help meet the needs of those particular children.

Government when It Struggles	Government when It Shines
• It lacks the financial and human resources to carry out its responsibilities effectively.	• Its own resources are multiplied by seeking and welcoming community partners, including communities of faith.
• Often being risk averse, government can tend to resist big change.	• It recognizes that success will require trying things that have not been done in that jurisdiction before.
• Bureaucratic complexity can drag out processes endlessly, ultimately leaving children and families waiting.	• It encourages its staff at all levels to maintain positive and productive relationships with community partners.
• Due to term limitations, elected officials may struggle to maintain a long-term view of foster care transformation.	• Knowing their time is limited, elected officials can give focus and urgency to child welfare improvements.

Government partnerships with faith communities can be powerful for both. Jedd Medefind, president of the Christian Alliance for Orphans, has said, "Without the Church, foster care is often just a cold system. Without foster care, the Church is often just a cold building."[39]

Government partnerships are not limited to child welfare administrators. You may also find yourself in partnership with elected officials both at a county and state level, even including the governor's office. The next page contains a list of pointers for those in the faith community, gathered from leaders in government.

Five Tips for Faith Communities from former Government Leaders

1. Demonstrate humility.

A stance of humility, graciousness, and genuine interest in the person always goes a long way—perhaps especially when the person is on the "other side of the fence" from you. Also, as you sense what matters a lot to the leader, you'll be able to connect your issue with their priorities.

2. Be succinct.

Be prepared to explain the problem and your proposals with few words. Pair this with a simple story or a visual—a chart or a physical object that "embodies" your message. This can make your message more understandable and hard to forget.

3. Be solutions oriented.

Bemoaning problems likely won't accomplish much unless you also present a positive vision for how change is possible. And even if you want government to do more, always include thoughts on what can be done outside of government. If possible, have a specific request in mind going into any meeting with a government official.

4. Be both innocent and shrewd.

Political leaders are pulled in many directions. Most genuinely want to make the world a better place, but they also need certain things to fuel their future work—including positive news stories about their efforts, support from organizations and networks, votes or financial support for their campaigns. You likely can't provide all of these things, but consider how their support for your proposals could be a "double win" for them.

5. Demonstrate your long-term commitment to the issue.

Some government leaders may be cautious about working with someone representing the faith community and may perceive that you will not stay engaged for long. Asking them about their previous experiences with the faith community might shed light on assumptions they have. It's essential to demonstrate your long-term commitment to the issue and to working collaboratively with them to find solutions.

2. Private Child Placement Agencies (CPAs)

In many states, the foster care system has chosen to contract with licensed private agencies to carry out tasks such as:

- Recruitment
- Training
- Family certification
- Child placement
- Family support and ongoing monitoring

If you are in a state that privatizes and of its foster care services, agencies are a vital ally in local foster care movement-building. They are subject matter experts in your community. They have a vested interest in knowing what works and what doesn't, and it would be foolish to overlook that experience. In most cases, they hold a government contract and are working to meet the objectives outlined in that contract.

It can be difficult for an agency to play the backbone role in a local collaborative movement. Other agencies and organizations may see them as a competitor and churches may see them merely as another community organization vying for its people's time and attention. They are generally perceived as an institution (potentially a very good one!) rather than a rallying point for movement. This is where a bridge organization (see the next section) can be invaluable. That said, it is hard to overstate the vital role of agencies in providing professional services that enable churches to become actively engaged. And while most any quality agency can fulfill this function, one that shares the faith commitments of local churches can play an especially vital part in recruiting, training, certifying, and supporting families.

Overall, an agency's ability to facilitate local movement building (beyond foster care activity) will be proportional to its ability to maintain a noncompetitive, openhanded posture as a servant of the collective vision of local churches.

Private Agencies when They Struggle	Private Agencies when They Shine
• Due to competition for government funds, can become territorial. • Their communications to churches may convey how the church can serve the agency's vision rather than how the agency can serve the church's vision.	• They take an "all ships rise on a rising tide" approach. • They seek the success of other agencies and organizations in the community through openhandedness, credit sharing, and collaboration. • They recognize that the collaboration of churches is vital to lasting local foster care movement, so they take the posture of a midwife—helping churches fulfill their calling.

3. Bridge Organizations

Over the past two decades, a new kind of organization has emerged to bridge the historical gap between faith communities and public child welfare institutions. In most cases, these "bridge organizations" have developed as groups of local churches collaborating to address foster care in their communities. Often, they operate informally for a while and eventually incorporate as official nonprofits. Some of them operate under the umbrella of a local church (though they represent several churches).

Perhaps the most significant distinction between a bridge organization and a private child placement agency is that bridge organizations do not place and supervise child placement in foster homes (a function that requires licensure and a state contract). They play many of the other roles that an agency might, but not placement. This makes it easier for a bridge organization to maintain a largely noncompetitive stance in a community. Their greatest asset may be their neutrality. When they lose that, they change the dynamics of how they serve, which may compromise their effectiveness.

In 2016, Taylor University conducted an exploratory study on several bridge organizations around the country to define their activities and structure more fully. The Taylor study found that:

- 89% of the bridge organizations surveyed are engaged in active recruitment for foster and adoptive families;

- 89% consider connecting churches to foster care as a focus of their work;
- 78% of participating organizations offered support services to foster and adoptive parents including support groups, mentoring, respite care training, parenting classes, and others;
- 100% focus on education and training (the participating organizations indicated their target education populations are the children [11%], caretakers [78%], churches [89%], and the community [89%]);
- 100% regularly pray for their foster care and adoptive families;
- 78% are currently involved in reforming [government] foster care policies; and
- 100% of the organizations partner with local government.

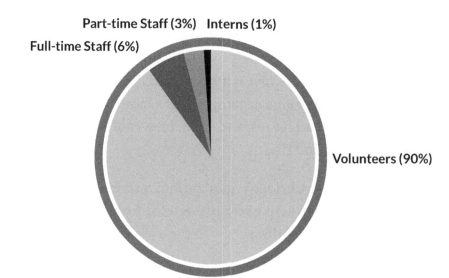

Part-time Staff (3%)   Interns (1%)
Full-time Staff (6%)
Volunteers (90%)

The vast majority are not receiving government funding and are primarily funded by private donors and by participating churches. They are largely volunteer driven. Among the organizations surveyed, volunteers made up 90 percent of the workforce of the surveyed bridge organizations.

In a more recent survey of bridge organizations, these five activities emerge as those that nearly every bridge organization surveyed participated in and saw as vital to their work:

1. Family recruitment (foster, adoptive, support)
2. Church engagement
3. Education and training
4. Social support of families
5. Government interaction

The bridge organization's ability to garner trust with both church and state is largely based on its ability to be bilingual, able to both understand and speak both church and state language and terminology. This allows them to play the role of translator, helping to introduce those in the faith community to critical work within child welfare and vise versa.

When our twin daughters were freshmen, they got their first introduction to Shakespeare through *Romeo and Juliet*. Their English teacher required a version that is part of the series, *No Fear Shakespeare*. On the left-hand side is the original text. On the right is a translation into modern language. Some of you are purists, and the very idea of this is offensive to you—maybe like serving caviar with Cheetos. However, I, for one, think it's fabulous (but agree that no one should ever ruin Cheetos with caviar).

Here is one of Romeo's passages in the original language:

> *Alack, there lies more peril in thine eye*
> *Than twenty of their swords.*
> *Look thou but sweet,*
> *And I am proof against their enmity.*[41]

Huh? Here it is for the Cheetos crowd:

> *Alas, one angry look from you would be worse*
> *than twenty of your relatives with swords.*
> *Just look at me kindly,*
> *and I'm invincible against their hatred.*[42]

I can appreciate the beauty of the original words, but I also really like understanding stuff. Translation is a beautiful thing. It's important not just because it leads to understanding, but also because it keeps people from casting good things aside. How many high school freshmen have sworn off Shakespeare for a lifetime because it seemed inaccessible? Having a good translator can make all the difference.

Among other things, this is one of the primary functions of a bridge organization. They are walking between the two different worlds of church and state. These are two worlds that, without translators, easily find ways to cast the other aside. Here are just a few key things that sometimes need translating:

- Helping the Church understand why child welfare professionals find the word "orphan" offensive when referring to kids in foster care
- Helping the state understand how biblical concept of caring for "orphans" is a central driving force in the Church community engaging in foster care even if kids are not technically orphans by the modern definition
- Helping the Church and state understand lingo and abbreviations inherent to the child welfare system and the church respectively
- Helping the Church understand that—although the fundamentals of healthy parenting doesn't change—special empathy, extra patience, and new tactics may be critical to parenting children who've experienced major trauma

The bridge organization can provide an important rallying point for churches and organizations in its community. It is nimble and may have more latitude, since its funding comes from donors, not government. There are also some important cautions to consider as well.

Bridge Organizations when They Struggle	Bridge Organizations when They Shine
• New leadership meets with government, rallies churches, creates excitement but does so without forming solid partnerships with existing players (agencies and service organizations). • Builds the organization around a single personality or couple. When things get busy or hard at home for that couple (who are often caring for kids from hard places), the momentum gained in the community can be lost. • Builds the organization (logo, branding, website) but loses its character as a "coalition of churches" working together. It ends up being another non-profit in the foster care space rather than the backbone of a local church-driven movement.	• See themselves first and foremost as empowering churches who are working together to address foster care effectively. • Develop a broad leadership team— including an active board (where applicable), staff, and volunteer structure that ensures its continuity for the foreseeable future. • Build honest and healthy lines of communication between church and state so that effective work can continue to thrive even when there are frictions. • Maintain their neutrality in the local space. They've effectively positioned themselves as an ally rather than as a competitor among other organizations.

4. Service Organizations

A nonprofit service organization provides one or more specific services related to children and families in foster care. They are usually somewhat specialized and are a vital part of a community that together offers all the services needed to provide *more than enough* for children and families. Here is a partial list of the services these organizations provide:

- Counseling
- Child care
- Legal advocacy (i.e., CASA)
- Addiction recovery
- Mentoring
- Foster closet
- Respite care
- Educational advocacy
- Parent training
- Equine therapy
- Family preservation host homes
- Aging out services

The beautiful thing about a collaborative community effort is that many of these services can be coordinated in a way they may never have been before. With this kind of coordination, you can ensure that every child or family can get connected to each of the resources they need. This increased efficiency can make a huge difference toward the overall goal of providing *more than enough.*

Service Organizations when They Struggle	Service Organizations when They Shine

• A program or service is created based on the assumptions of the organizational leader rather than on a deep understanding of the real needs of foster care in a community (i.e., "we will give every child in foster care a toothbrush, whether they need one or not!").
 	
 • They are not able to articulate how their product or service helps children achieve what they most need and long for: connection, felt safety, and permanency.
	• They are always asking …
	  ○ What do children and families in our community need most?
	  ○ Why are we providing the things we are providing?
	  ○ Who are the people experiencing life change as a result of the products or services we offer, and how can we continue to serve them better?
	
	 • They see themselves as part of an ensemble cast of organizations and churches in a community rather than as an end in themselves. This comes across in how they work with others, as well as in their donor communications, website, and social media.

5. Local Businesses

An often-overlooked source for community transformation is local business. While this certainly can and
often does include financial provision for a local effort, it
can be so much more. Local businesses can provide jobs
and job training for teens in foster care and aging out
youth. Meanwhile, the thoughtful guidance or mentorship
of a business person can be a game changer for a young
person who may not have had a relationship like that in
his or her life.

Businesses can contribute in other ways as well. For
example, their communications platforms can raise the
visibility of a community effort in a huge way. And specific
services offered by these businesses—from lawyers to
barbers, orthodontists to mechanics—can be invaluable
in supporting foster youth and families.

A local adoption event in our community held twice a
year draws 150 to 250 people each time. A local restaurant
owner has furnished a fantastic dinner for every one of
these events for years now. When a local business puts
its weight behind foster care, it can have enormous long-
term impact.

Local Businesses when They Struggle	Local Businesses when They Shine
• They simply don't know where or how they can contribute. • Businesses may presume that the principles that make them a successful business will always translate to local nonprofit organizations. • They leverage financial contribution to drive strategies without seeking the wisdom of those with more experience in child welfare. • Energy is directed toward efforts that have popular appeal (positive PR) but minimal strategic impact.	• They are thoughtfully guided in regard to specific ways their unique gifts could be well used. • Applicable experience from starting and growing a business is humbly applied to a local nonprofit effort while recognizing the differences between for-profit and non-for-profit endeavors. • They recognize stewardship responsibilities to make wise investments in things that truly help children and families. • They seek the insight of local and national experts and rely on those insights when deciding how to engage with a problem. • They look for ways to engage in solutions that require not only their financial investment, but also their expertise, and perhaps other resources from their employees and business.

From "Who?" to "How?"

Now that we've explored who the ensemble cast is, the rest of the book will discuss the question of how to travel well with them. How do we work through their areas of struggle and celebrate it when they shine? What does it look like for a group of passionate, gifted, quirky, and flawed people to work together collaboratively and provide *more than enough* for children and families in your community?

It begins with building trust.

As we mentioned earlier, organizations don't collaborate, people do. Essentially, this means that you cannot collaborate without some level of trust, and trust cannot be built without relationship. Relationship cannot be established without spending time together.

While there are no shortcuts to building trust, there are things that can help facilitate it. At the Christian Alliance for Orphans, we see one of our roles in the body of Christ as creating environments where leaders can build trust, share ideas, and collaborate to make a bigger difference together than they could make by themselves. We are always looking for tools and ideas that help this process. One of the most helpful tools I've come across is a set of principles we learned from North Point Church just outside of Atlanta.

Lesli Reece, who leads the foster care ministry there, put together a document for their partnerships. Every time Lesli begins a relationship with another organization, she signs a document that contains these principles and tells them that these are the things she is committing to in that relationship. A version of these principles for your use can be found on the following page:

Fostering Trust

Out of my care for you and the work we do, these are four commitments I am making to you, as we work together. Even if our collaborative effort comes to an end, these principles will continue to govern my individual conduct toward you.

1. When there's a gap between what I expected and what I experienced, I will fill in that gap with trust rather than suspicion. If that gap begins to erode my trust, I'll come straight to you.
2. When I have doubts that I will be able to deliver on a promise, I will tell you right away.
3. When you confront me about the gaps I have created, I will be honest and transparent with you.
4. When other people assume the worst about you, I will speak positively about you and encourage them to talk directly to you.

Signed _____

Date _____

*These principles were adapted from a message by Andy Stanley. If you'd like to go deeper on this topic, the full message can be found on the Trust vs. Suspicion: How to create and maintain a culture of trust in your organization DVD or Digital Download. These are available for purchase at store.northpoint.org.

Leslie does not ask the other person to sign the document. She is merely communicating the principles that will govern her own actions. Sometimes people appreciate it. Sometimes people aren't sure what to think (after all, most people aren't accustomed to this kind of transparency). On one occasion, Lesli gave the document to an administrator with the county. She was one of the people that wasn't sure what to make of it. But she took it and went on with the conversation. Months later, this administrator approached Lesli and told her that based on that document, she had something she needed to talk about. She had been at one of the events the church was hosting and overheard a foster mom sharing details of a case with another woman there. She was concerned that maybe this woman was breaking confidentiality. When they investigated further, however, they quickly learned the other woman was part of that foster family's support community and was officially cleared to receive those details. Problem solved.

Without these principles governing the relationship, it's easy to imagine what might have happened instead. This administrator might have gone to her colleagues and shared how members of the church were breaking confidentiality. Eventually, that could have grown into something much larger that destroyed the partnership altogether. That kind of thing happens all the time and has sabotaged many collaborative efforts. This, of course, has tragic consequences for the children and families that could have benefited from those efforts. We owe it to the children in our community to protect our collaborative relationships with others. They depend on us to act like adults.

Collaboration Done Well

When it's done correctly, this ensemble cast can together transform foster care in a community. They serve with a shared vision and a commitment to building trust with one another. They set aside some of what they don't agree on to focus on the things they do agree on. They understand the problem is too big to solve alone and that only the foolish try to do so. Collaborative movements are defined by an atmosphere of generosity and a relentless commitment to resolving conflict biblically and looking beyond differences. If you are waiting to collaborate until you find someone more like you, you are missing the point of collaboration. Our kids and families need what you have to offer, but they also need someone who has gifts and perspectives that you don't have. Collaboration done well can change everything.

chapter eleven
Villains of Foster Care

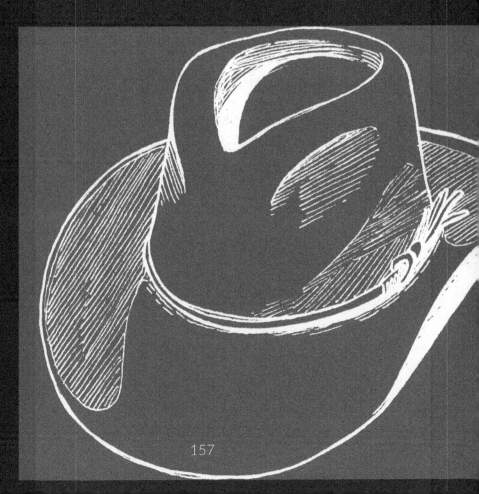

"When I'm ready to fight, my opponent has a better chance of surviving a forest fire wearing gasoline drawers."

—Mr. T

E very story has a villain. And the way we fight them changes depending on who the villain is:

Villain	How You Fight Them
Darth Vader (Star Wars [43])	Lightsaber
Jaws (Jaws [44])	Exploding scuba tank
Count Rugen (Princess Bride [45])	Sword (while saying "My name is Inigo Montoya. You killed my father. Prepare to die.")
Warden Norton (Shawshank Redemption [46])	Administrative paperwork (sent to the local newspaper)
Biff Tannen (Back to the Future [47])	A George McFly left cross
Scar (The Lion King [48])	Traitorous Hyenas
The Wicked Witch of the West (The Wizard of Oz [49])	A bucket of water ("I'm melting!)

This goes beyond movies, of course. If the villain is a mouse in your house, your approach will be different than if it is wayward wasp. Hopefully.

Who you fight dictates how you fight.

When it comes to foster care, the way we answer the question, "Who is the villain?" is incredibly important. Who we see as the villain changes how we approach foster care. Here are three common ways people have traditionally answered the "villain question" and the harmful resulting postures of each:

Villain #1: Biological Parents

There are certainly people out there whose actions can be described as nothing short of evil. However, most children are in foster care due to things like neglect as a result of poverty, lack of education, and drug or alcohol addiction. The mistreatment of a child is never justified, but we mustn't allow ourselves to see these parents as villains. Their actions are correctable, and these moms and dads are just as redeemable as you and I are in our brokenness.

I asked some foster parents about whether their perspectives on biological parents have changed over time. Their answers are telling. Here are just a few:

> "I will never forget the moment God changed my heart about the birth parents. I was sitting in court. I had pictures of the baby we were fostering. . . . I had them in my hands, and I was looking at them when the mom came into court in handcuffs and ankle shackles wearing an orange jumpsuit. Hard to believe that 'terrible' woman had given birth to this 'beautiful' baby. I wanted to hate her. I gave the pics to her lawyer, who handed them to her. She turned to me with tears in her eyes and mouthed, "Thank you." At that moment, God said to me, 'I love her as much as I love that sweet innocent baby. I created her. You need to show her as much love as you show this child.'" —Jennifer

"My perspective changed from fear to sympathy and support with each biological family member I met. It is easier to be scared of things you don't know, to villainize someone because you don't know their story. Meeting with family members (immediate or extended family) and just listening to them was by far the most effective tool in softening my heart and fears." —Amanda

"I was intimidated at first and wanted to jump on the wagon of placing blame because they were the reason their kids were in care. Over time I realized something needed to change to break the cycle, so I started being a resource for the biological family. . . . Everyone makes bad choices, and we all have people who have rallied in our corner to make sure we stayed on the right path." —Crystal

When we see biological parents (or other family members) as the villains of foster care, it changes how we approach foster care in our communities. We tend to become exclusively focused on adoption. We create an "us versus them" environment in our support groups. We teach our foster parents to be fearful rather than train them to seek God's best for everyone involved. As a result, children who could go home to the parents they love might not get to. And parents who would thrive if given a second chance might not get one. This is not to say that termination of parental rights is never appropriate and that adoption is never needed. They are. But for many kids and their parents, we could do so much better. It all starts with loving them as Jesus calls us to—as ourselves, and not vilifying them.

Villain #2: The Foster Care System Itself

My wife, out of her deep love for our family and her desire for us all to live long and happy lives, works hard to introduce us to healthy food. I genuinely appreciate this. If left to myself, I'd have Chipotle burritos, chicken fingers, mac and cheese, and chocolate milk nearly every meal (not all at once, of course . . . well, maybe).

However, last year she tried out a new recipe for making kale chips. She mixed up a bunch of seasonings, dumped it all over a pile of kale leaves on a baking sheet and put it in the oven . . . to wilt . . . on purpose. This makes the house smell terrible. I love my wife, but I do not love the smell of hot, wilting kale.

When these leafy little morsels were perfectly singed, they were removed from the oven. The first time they came out, I would have bet the house AND a Chipotle burrito that those things would sit on the counter untouched until they had to be thrown away days later. And then, even the neighborhood rabbits (who eat *everything*) would avoid our part of the alley where the trash can sits.

But something strange happened. The kids started eating them. Not only did they eat them, they *loved* them. They even came home from school sometimes and asked if they could make kale chips. On more than one occasion, the smell has awoken one of my older daughters from a teenage coma to stumble downstairs and exclaim, "Kale chips!?"

The dog even begs for them. Traitor.

I genuinely don't understand it. Kale chips are terrible. They smell and taste bad. Nobody should eat these things. And certainly, nobody should love them.

There are a lot of people who see the foster care system the same way I see kale chips. They see it as exclusively terrible. They see it as something to be discarded. They talk about how it hurts kids, destroys families, and abuses the foster parents who are trying to help. They say it stinks.

The thing is, many of those statements are often true. The foster care system and its brokenness sometimes contribute to lifelong pain for thousands. The system can have a certain unsavory smell that is often repulsive. And nothing I write here is meant to minimize that in any way.

But, it's important to hold another reality in tension at the same time. It is this same system that protects children every day, saving lives, and also creates environments where hurting and broken adults can get help for addictions and get access to resources they've never had before. Yes, there are not-so-great foster parents and not-so-great social workers. You hear about them in the news all the time (just set up a google alert for the phrase "foster care" and you will see). But there are also tens of thousands of good, faithful foster parents, child welfare professionals, and service providers who are delivering healing by the truckload and aren't making the news.

It's okay to say that the system is falling short and then try to do something to help. However, there are a lot of kids and families who are safe and thriving because of what the system—or rather the people in the system—have provided.

So how does it change things when we stop seeing the system as the villain and consider things from this perspective? Here are two thoughts:

1. We can acknowledge that, while the system may be broken, the professionals in it need and deserve our support. They are doing vital work in the toughest of environments. Many of them are as frustrated as anyone about the shortcomings of the system in which they work. Write a kind note, take a worker to lunch, and provide the support that gives them the strength not only to endure, but to make things better.

2. Often, when we see holes in the system, we say, "*They* ought to fix that." When we find value in the system rather than just deficiency, it makes it easier for us to ask, "Is there something *we* can do to help?" After all, these are kids and families that our churches are trying to love with the love of Jesus. *We* have a job to do. All over the country, churches are stepping into these holes without judgment. They are making a real difference for kids and families. Wouldn't it make sense for us to try to help improve the systems we are asking these churches to step into?

I still don't like kale chips, but watching my daughter inhale them reminds me that I don't know everything. There's another side to things, and it's helping my family be healthier.

Villain #3: Other Organizations

Many of us view another organization or agency in our community as the villain in foster care. We don't like their arrogance. We don't like the way they have treated someone in our church. We don't like their philosophy of caring for kids. We don't like the way they do that certain program. We don't like their theology. We don't like that they are taking donor dollars that could be used for our excellent programs and are using them for their mediocre ones. We don't like the way they aren't strategic enough. We don't like that they seem like they are only out for personal gain. We don't like the fact that they don't like us. We don't like *them*. Things would be better without them. Now that you've had a paragraph to consider it, I'll bet somebody or some organization may have come to mind for you.

> **When we see other people providing services for children and families as the villain, we collectively become too small to solve the foster care crisis in our community.**

When we see other people providing services for children and families as the villain, we collectively become too small to solve the foster care crisis in our community. You don't have to like everything about someone else providing services. You don't even have to refer people there. But you should figure out a way to work together when it makes sense for the well-being of kids and families in your community. How? It comes down to a commitment to building relationships.

I was recently in a meeting with two leaders of two different Christian foster care agencies operating in the same city. In many contexts, "Jim" and "Mike" would be considered competitors. They partner with the same types of churches, approach the same types of donors, and recruit the same types of families. Jim was approached by a local church in their community and told that they wanted to start partnering with him because they were not happy with Mike's organization.

> **We are not just responsible to see *that* good things get done, but as followers of Jesus, we are also responsible for *how* good things get done.**

Jim said that while his organization would be happy to serve their church, he wasn't willing to do that until the church had a conversation with Mike to try and work things out. The three of them met, and the misunderstanding was resolved. To this day, that church continues to be a strong partner for Mike's organization. It is making a difference for children and families. Jim's organization could have easily taken the partnership, and the church would still be making a huge difference. However, we are not just responsible to see *that* good things get done, but as followers of Jesus, we are also responsible for *how* good things get done.

So what is the root reason this was able to happen? Well, first, Jim and Mike both love Jesus and are committed to doing things the way He wants them to. Secondly, they have a relationship with each other. They don't always agree about how things should be done. But they are committed to maintaining unity in the body of Christ. That unity is built on trust that is born out of relationship.

The Real Villains of Foster Care

So if the biological parents, the system, and other organizations are not the villains of foster care, who are? At the most basic level, we, as Christians, believe that there are evil spiritual forces at work in this world. These forces desire to *"steal and kill and destroy"* (John 10:10). They seek to destroy children and families through addiction, anger, violence, lust, and greed. They try to keep the church on the sidelines rather than loving their neighbor. These sinister enemies produce a myriad of things for us to fight against. But when we turn away, even momentarily from fighting against these true enemies to fight against other people—other image-bearers of God Himself—we become vulnerable.

Ephesians 6:12 tells us, *"Our struggle is not against flesh and blood, but against the rulers, against the authorities, against the powers of this dark world and against the spiritual forces of evil in the heavenly realms."*

Fighting each other becomes a distraction that only serves to remove us from our highest place of impact for children and families. Children are suffering from real evils. When we expend energy fighting other people who are trying to help, we prolong and even worsen the suffering of children in our communities. And for what?

If we fight Darth Vader with a lightsaber and we fight the Wicked Witch of the West with a bucket of water, then what is the right way to fight our enemy? If we believe our enemy is flesh and blood, we will fight with angry words, slander, gossip, and contempt. But if it's true that spiritual forces oppose our efforts to help children, then our primary weapons become prayer and all things rooted in the good counsel of Scripture: love, joy, peace, patience, kindness, goodness, faithfulness, gentleness, and self-control (Galatians 5:22–23). *Who* you fight dictates *how* you fight.

> **When we expend energy fighting other people who are trying to help, we prolong and even worsen the suffering of children in our communities. And for what?**

We must fight the right enemy using the right weapons.

chapter twelve
Invading Someone's Bubble

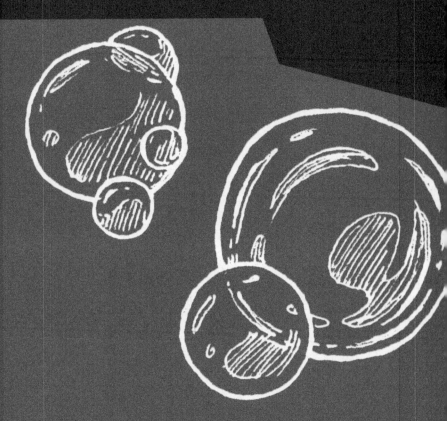

169

"Get off my lawn."

—Someone you might know

When one of our daughters (who is now a teenager and has approved this chapter) was little, she tended to invade people's personal space. She had developed some sensory issues and was always seeking sensory input. From dragging her hands across the entire length of the glass case at the supermarket deli to spinning around incessantly, she was always looking for ways to get her sensory needs met. When we had guests over, she would sit right up next to them (or on top of them) and touch their face and hair. There's nothing that says "welcome to our home" quite like a three-year-old you don't know squeezing your cheeks together and petting you like a cat. One of the most common words you would hear us say to her was "bubble." That was our gentle reminder that she had entered into someone else's "bubble" without their permission.

> **There's nothing that says "welcome to our home" quite like a three-year-old you don't know squeezing your cheeks together and petting you like a cat.**

There is a relatively new reality in Christian foster care that has developed over the past two decades. In many areas in multiple states, there are many churches focused on foster care as well as Christian nonprofit bridge organizations and agencies rallying around those churches and connecting them to the state. Also, there are national organizations that are implementing programs and hosting events in a number of localities in various states. Said simply, there are a lot more Christians doing a lot more great work in foster care than ever before. That is fantastic news!

But another reality can come with that. Sometimes folks can feel like their "bubble" is being invaded by another ministry, church, or organization. Maybe you've been teaching churches how to develop foster care ministries, and now another organization has come into town doing the same thing. Perhaps your donor base has begun giving to other organizations that have popped up. Maybe you feel another organization's work isn't quite as effective as yours and is diverting people away from more strategic activity.

So now what?

Here are a few things for each side of this equation to consider:

To those "invading"...

- Recognize that you weren't there first, and with that reality comes additional responsibility. If you are entering a community, you have a responsibility to know who else is working there, what they are doing, and how your work may impact them. You also must be very careful with the vision you are casting as to why you are entering that community. To cast a vision that suggests "we are entering this community because there is no one here doing the work that we do" is potentially damaging, prideful, and counterproductive.

- Be a learner. Just because your message or your program has been effective in other places doesn't mean it will work the same here. There may be small tweaks that will help more kids and families. The best way to find out is to talk to the leaders that have been there longer than you.

- Your very presence in the community may be raising the anxiety level of your brothers and sisters in Christ. You do not have the option of seeing that as their problem. There is too much work to do, and you need each other to do it well. You are a part of God's family before you are a foster care advocate. Family first. In humility, have the conversations you need to have and stay committed to unity.

To those "being invaded" . . .

- Unless there are already *more than enough* foster families, adoptive families, services for biological families, and family supports in your community, you need help. It's probably safe to say that there is not yet *more than enough* where you live. When you compete with or resent other organizations, it is the equivalent of saying, "our work is enough to get the job done." There are kids and families in your community right now that you are failing to help. That's not a criticism, it's just a reminder that you could probably use an invader or two to help out.

- Having others working for the same goals will make you both better. We all produce better work when we hang out with and encourage other people doing great work. As mentioned earlier, treat other ministries and organizations like workout partners, not members of a different team. Members of different teams look for strategic and calculated ways to beat each other. Workout partners cheer each other on, spot each other, and push one another toward better things. You are partners in this.

To both the "invaders" and the "invaded" . . .

- As we established in the last chapter, "Our struggle is not against flesh and blood, but against the rulers, against the authorities, against the powers of this dark world and against the spiritual forces of evil in the heavenly realms" (Ephesians 6:12). There are forces that desperately want you to fail your mission. If you find yourself locked into a battle with other people trying to help kids and families in your community, those forces are winning. We have a common enemy, and it's not one another.
- When these feelings of violation or competition come up, it's not a relational problem. It's not primarily a ministry strategy problem. It's a theological problem. We are choosing to live according to our flesh rather than according to commands God has given us in Scripture concerning unity, humility,

and love. The theology we know in our heads is not being lived out in our hearts and actions.

- If you are telling others about the weaknesses of another organization and have never had that conversation with them, that is wrong. Remember, there are people outside the church who are watching. Secular organizational leaders have observed Christians in the foster care space treating each other poorly at times, and it has caused them to back away from partnership. That's messed up, my friends.

- Whether you are the "invader" or the "invaded," you have the responsibility to take the first step. Many battles can be avoided, and many more children can be helped if you will take out your phone, call the person you've been thinking about as you've read these last couple of chapters, and ask them to lunch.

> **I believe that our unity is more important to God than our impact. And by the way, if we practice unity, our impact will be far greater than we could have ever imagined.**

The bottom line is that we have to stay committed to talking to each other. This is about God's kingdom. When we work as a unified team against a common enemy, our victorious celebration will be sweet. I believe that our unity is more important to God than our impact. And by the way, if we practice unity, our impact will be far greater than we could have ever imagined.

chapter thirteen
Credit Check

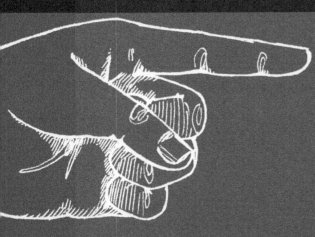

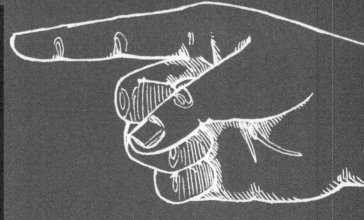

"It is amazing what you can accomplish
if you do not care who gets the credit."

—Harry S. Truman

n 2018, Jason Witten, the tight end for the Dallas Cowboys retired. While he has since returned to football, the retirement press conference held by his coach, Jason Garret, stands as an instructive moment for us all. And despite some of the jargon, you won't need to understand football to catch it.

Coach Garret was paying tribute to Jason Witten when he told a story about their 2015 training camp. The coach had asked some of their veteran players to prepare a presentation for the rest of the team. Witten chose to do his presentation on a single play called "Y Option." Coach Garret shared that this is Jason Witten's signature play. Witten has over eleven hundred career catches, and half of them likely came from this one play. Coach Garret went on to describe Witten's presentation:

> "He talked about his stance, where his weight is, where his hand is . . . He talked about his eyes, his shoulders, hips, his feet, the angle he's taking coming out, what he's doing with the ball after he catches it. It was just like nothing I'd ever seen."
>
> Witten then showed the team a clip from a playoff game the previous season against Detroit. The Cowboys were down by three points with just over six minutes left in the game. It was fourth down with six yards to go for the first down. The entire season was on the line with this

one play. When Quarterback Tony Romo approached the line of scrimmage, he saw the defense's formation and changed the play to Y Option by yelling out the code word "Tennessee." The ball was snapped, and Witten released downfield. He opted to cut inside (something he only did one out of a hundred times on this play) and caught the pass and ran for the first down. A few plays later, they scored a touchdown and won the game to advance.

After showing this clip to his teammates, Witten talked about the things he saw out there and how it all felt. He then stopped and said to his team, "I'll tell you why this play really worked."

Witten said, "I want you to look at Dez Bryant here. He's our best receiver. They played two-man for one reason: Dez Bryant. Dez Bryant is one of the best receivers in the national football league. He deserves that attention."

Then he talked about the offensive line—Tyron Smith and his set and how he used his hands and where his eyes were and how he punched and scratched and clawed and fought. He talked about Ron Lira, our left guard, Travis Frederick and Zack Martin working inside, working together. He talked about Jeremy Parnell, our right tackle, his set, and how he was battling to somehow keep the rusher away from Romo. He talked about Cole Beasley and Terrance Williams taking outside releases, turning the defender's eyes away from him and running the safety off so he'd be isolated. He talked about DeMarco Murray, his protection assignment, running a swing, get that linebacker *out of there so I can break inside. Then he talked about Romo. The greatness of Romo—his toughness, mental toughness, physical toughness, his instincts, his awareness to kind of hang in there with him. It all came alive on fourth and six. Romo slid, threw it between the eight and the two, and he went. So it struck me, that this play—his signature play, where he made it at the critical moment—he didn't make it about him. He did what he always does. He made it about everybody else. He made it about the team.[50]*

> **What if, when faced with an opportunity to tell a crowd, a donor, a state administrator, or an elected official how effective our work is, we made sure to bring up our friends and partners who make us more effective?**

People often associate professional athletes with ego and self-interest. However, I find it fascinating how good so many of them are at sharing credit with others. You will often see great athletes at press conferences fielding questions about game-changing plays they made. Very often, they simply divert credit to someone else on their team who made it possible. While the most cynical among us might attribute this to excellent media training, there are some valuable lessons for us to learn.

What if we were known for this same thing? What if, when faced with an opportunity to tell a crowd, a donor, a state administrator, or an elected official how effective our work is, we made sure to bring up our friends and partners who make us more effective?

One organization I know of introduced one of their large donors to another ministry they felt the donor might want to give to. Their focus was not "how do I get a donor and keep them." Rather, it was "how do we help this donor give according to their passions and leverage their resources for maximum kingdom impact." Instead of accumulating donors, they are serving them. Fast-forward several years, and that donor is giving more to each organization than they ever did for the first one.

I recently spoke with the leader of a large national network who has been observing nonprofits for many years. He noted that the organizations that, from the very beginning, were most openhanded with others concerning donors and resources are the organizations that continue to thrive the most to this day. He noted that the converse of that was true as well. Organizations that seemed overly concerned about territory and control at the beginning have had the hardest time. There is one thing that donors find even more inspiring than organizations that do great work—organizations that are strategic enough to collaborate with others to make a more significant impact.

While credit sharing accomplishes a lot of things, there are three in particular that are important to note:

1. Credit sharing increases trust.

In a 2017 Harvard Business Review article, entitled "The Neuroscience of Trust," Paul J. Zak writes, "The neuroscience shows that recognition has the largest effect on trust when it occurs immediately after a goal has been met, when it comes from peers, and when it's tangible, unexpected, personal, and public."[51]

When we publicly recognize others, it helps to build trust between us. It shows visibly that we trust them enough to draw attention to their work and that we believe they will be faithful with that attention. It also causes them to trust us as a team player who has their best interests in mind. Trust is the engine oil of collaboration. As long as you have it, your partnership with others can go far. But if it begins to leak and you run out, not only will you stop moving forward, you'll ruin your engine. When we point out the great things our partners have done, we are adding oil to the engine. It is a reconfirmation that you are not in this for your own glory and that you can be trusted with success.

> **Trust is the engine oil of collaboration. As long as you have it, your partnership with others can go far. But if it begins to leak and you run out, not only will you stop moving forward, you'll ruin your engine.**

Nothing destroys trust like feeling that someone is out for their own personal gain. That kind of self-interest is ugly on everyone. There are lots of things that can build trust (keeping your promises, telling the truth, etc.), but sharing credit is near the top of the list.

2. Credit sharing is truth telling.

When we share the credit with others, we are not exhibiting some kind of false humility or employing an empty form of flattery to make that person more loyal to us. Sharing credit is truth telling. It is merely the act of recognizing out loud what is actually true: you didn't do this thing by yourself. If you believe you did, you are delusional. If you know you didn't but pretend you did, you are worse than delusional. When you are in the midst of a collaborative effort, just be honest about how things are getting done. It will go a long way.

There was a recent panel discussion at a conference in Washington, D.C., hosted by the Children's Bureau. The panel was about faith-based engagement in foster care and the audience was almost entirely made up of representatives from state agencies. The panel was comprised of three faith leaders and three government agency counterparts that they had been collaborating with. In some cases, these partnerships had been going on for years. It was a beautiful thing to watch these three sets of people who had achieved a great deal of success in foster care recruitment and support sit up there and give credit to one another for their success. They were honest about how apprehensive they were at first, and they were generous with their praise. People in our state governments are not always accustomed to being honored for their work, and in a secular state environment, people of faith are not always held up as examples to emulate. On this day, both happened.

3. Credit sharing strengthens your allies

The world can be a brutal place. The most confident person you know is still thirsty for encouragement. When we point out the great things others have done publicly, it serves as an encouragement to them. The word "encourage" comes from the French word "encoragier," which means to "make strong, hearten"[52] When we offer this kind of public encouragement to our allies, it makes them stronger. And all of us need to be as strong as possible to do what we are called to do.

> Sharing credit is truth telling. It is merely the act of recognizing out loud what is actually true: you didn't do this thing by yourself. If you believe you did, you are delusional. If you know you didn't but pretend you did, you are worse than delusional.

Our very first foster care case nearly twenty years ago involved two medically fragile preemie twin girls (just for the record, our paperwork said we were open to one kiddo with no major medical needs). The case took three-and-a-half years, involved the termination of parental rights, and ended in us adopting them. We had worked with somewhere in the neighborhood of fifteen professionals and another bunch of supportive friends. These included the caseworker, a parenting trainer for the biological mom, lawyers, doctors, nurses, physical therapists, and others. Many of them had been in our home numerous times and we had become so appreciative of how they had invested in our girls' lives. We wanted to do something small to demonstrate our gratitude so we reserved a room at the Old Spaghetti Factory in Denver and invited all of them to come for dinner on adoption day. To be honest, we thought that these folks probably got invited to a lot of things like this given the large number of kids they'd all served over the years. We were a pleasantly surprised that nearly all of them showed up! We created a document for everyone in attendance that listed each person and what their involvement had meant to us and our girls. Our only hope was to highlight their contribution and encourage them a little bit.

At the end, one social worker who had been involved mostly in the first year of our case working with bio mom told us, "I have been in child welfare for almost thirty years, and tonight is the best thing I've ever been a part of professionally. I don't ever get to see things on this side of a case."

Yes, but How?

Credit sharing isn't just a tool to pull out when you need it. It is habit-worthy and something you can get better at with practice. There is a fine line here between credit sharing and false humility. False humility devalues your own contribution to a thing to look humble.[53] For example, one might say, "We really didn't have anything to do with it— our friends at the State did all the heavy lifting." While this might appear humble, its lack of honesty is transparent. Instead, you might want to say, "We are really excited about what has happened through our partnership with the state. They have been an incredible ally as we fight for kids and families." Credit sharing simply tells the truth about others' contributions to provide a more accurate and complete picture of reality.

The good news is that we can practice it anywhere. It doesn't always need to be in front of large audiences. You can share credit when you are talking to your spouse, coworkers, or anyone else. Here are just a few examples to get you started:

> "I love your new haircut!"
> You: "Thank you! My stylist, Melanie, is fantastic."
>
> "You are such a good listener."
> You: "That's kind of you to say. I've learned a lot about that from watching my wife interact with others."
>
> "This event was amazing!"
> You: "I'm so glad you enjoyed it. You know, Tim over at First Community Church was terrific at pulling so many details together."

The person you bring up may never know you mentioned them. Even if that's true, you are becoming a stronger leader and the kind of person that others will love collaborating with. Credit sharing will bring strength to any collaborative effort. Your example will create a culture of credit sharing in your community, and you will all be better for it. More importantly, it will create the kind of culture that maximizes impact on children and families. Most importantly, it honors God and brings glory to Him.

chapter fourteen
Knowing Better and Doing Better

"Do the best you can until you know better, then when you know better, do better."

—Maya Angelou

was a child of the '80s. I was raised on Trapper Keepers, mixtapes, and scratch 'n' sniff stickers. I even remember when Honey Smacks were more accurately still called Sugar Smacks (according to a 2008 study, they are more than 50 percent sugar by weight—no kidding).[54]

And I had a mullet—business up front, party in the back.

One could argue that the mullet is a timeless hair fashion. Archaeologists have discovered evidence of the mullet in ancient Mesopotamia, Syria, Egypt, and Greece dating back as far as the sixteenth century BC.[55]

So while the '80s didn't invent the mullet, our generation rediscovered its ancient glory.

Many of us carried the mullet into the early '90s as well. I entered college as a music major with a mullet on my head and a leather jacket on my back. Yes, I was a living, breathing cliché. Then, after my freshman year, I went to California for a summer-long missions experience. Part of the deal was that we all had to find a summer job within the first two weeks of arriving. One of my very first interviews was at a fast-food place. "You have the job . . . but you will have to cut your hair."

Thanks, but no thanks. The mullet stays.

Several days passed and then a week. I still didn't have a job. I was from Kansas, and it was surprising to me that California, of all places, didn't seem to have an appreciation for hip hair. As the job deadline approached, I was beginning to come to grips with my fate. I had an interview at a Jack in the Box, and predictably, I was told, "You have the job . . . but you will have to cut your hair."

Uncle.

Watching several inches of hair fall to the floor of the barbershop didn't prove to be nearly as devastating as I might have thought. I got used to the change pretty quickly. My girlfriend didn't even dump me for a guy with cooler hair (in fact, she eventually married me). Every once in a while, we reach a point in life where we realize it is time for the mullet to go.

Maya Angelou said, "Do the best you can until you know better. Then when you know better, do better."

Nearly every one of us enter the foster care world naively. We come in with many preconceived ideas. From the moment we make the very first phone call to ask how to apply to be a foster parent, we begin to slowly and steadily have our assumptions dismantled. We are excited and willing to help kids who are waiting for help. We assume the person on the other end of the phone is going to be just as excited to receive our help. Surely, they will call us back right away and tell us how wonderful it is to receive our call. And then there is the paperwork that seems more geared toward keeping people out than letting people in. Then comes the training where it sure sounds like they are trying to talk folks out of this whole thing. Next, the kids show up, and, over time, their preciousness exceeds our expectations as does the manifestations of the trauma they have experienced. We brace ourselves to meet their monstrous biological parents only to find they are broken people like us. They are just adult versions of their precious children, looking for ways to heal themselves of their childhood wounds.

The same is true for those that enter into the child welfare profession. Every day holds a new reminder that this whole thing is not exactly what we thought it was going to be. Change comes harder than ever expected, and our enthusiasm seems to have less effect on justice than we had once dreamed.

> **We brace ourselves to meet their monstrous biological parents only to find they are broken people like us. They are just adult versions of their precious children, looking for ways to heal themselves of their childhood wounds.**

The more experienced we become, the less we know. This easily and all-too-often leads to cynicism and burnout. But it doesn't have to.

We can either say "nothing works" and resign ourselves to diminishing hope, or we can choose to say, "maybe it's not working because we didn't do it the right way." Every one of these disappointments can be a building block of experience that helps us to know better and then do better. The good old days are not always that good if we think about them. Occasionally, it becomes clear that it is time to move on to better things. We realize that it is time for the mullet to go.

Here are several examples of how we know better than we once did, and now we can do better:

- We know now that advocating for specific children with the people who already know them is a better way to recruit than putting up a billboard on the side of the interstate. This means finding as many family and community connections for a specific child as possible—teachers, coaches, distant relatives—and enlisting their help in identifying a potentially permanent home for a child.

- We know now that the language we use in recruitment can sometimes attract folks looking to rescue kids from "bad" families and put them into "good" families. We can change that. We can instead recruit potential foster families that are passionate about coming alongside biological families to bring restoration and reinforce those relationships.

- We know now that half of all foster families won't last a year unless they are surrounded by people who love them and support them. So let's not sign them on until we help them get the support they need.

- We know now that the behaviors of our children are very often the result of the traumatic things they have experienced. This shouldn't cause us to abandon structure, expectations, and discipline, but rather it should help us to add empathy and understanding to these things.

When we know better, we do better.

What to Do with People Who Don't Know Better

For those of us that have been in this for a while, there is also another side. When new people come along, we have to be exceedingly careful not to despise them for being naive like we once were. The temptation is to give in to cynicism and dismiss them. The right thing to do is to remember that we were there once, and we needed others to come beside us and help us grow. Here are a few examples you may be familiar with:

- When someone suggests to you that they've always wanted to build an orphanage for kids in foster care, don't get judgy on them. Gently guide them in what we know now about the importance of family. They are a potential ally for you to help kids and families. They are at least thinking about helping kids—remember, that's not true of everyone.

- When a couple calls about foster parenting and asks for babies under one year old, don't coldly turn them away and tell them there are only older kids in foster care. You have the chance to help this couple grow in their understanding and potentially help a child they never dreamed would be in their home.

- When someone says they couldn't do foster care because they couldn't deal with the birth families, don't write them off. Plenty of people have completely changed their philosophies about birth families after a single interaction with a birth mom.

This is so important in building local movement. Your team of advocates and volunteers are going to be a ragtag group of passionate people who may not yet know any better. That's okay. I am reminded of the story of Apollos as told in the book of Acts:

> *A Jew named Apollos, a native of Alexandria, came to Ephesus. He was a learned man, with a thorough knowledge of the Scriptures. He had been instructed in the way of the Lord, and he spoke with great fervor and taught about Jesus accurately, though he knew only the baptism of John. He began to speak boldly in the synagogue. When Priscilla and Aquila heard him, they invited him to their home and explained to him the way of God more adequately. When Apollos wanted to go to Achaia, the brothers and sisters encouraged him and wrote to the disciples there to welcome him. (Acts 18:24–27)*

What a beautiful example Priscilla and Aquila have given us of gentle correction and discipleship. In contrast, we tend to walk around with a "virtual trapdoor" button at the ready. When we encounter someone who says something off, we hit the button, open the virtual trapdoor, and have them removed quickly. We are gardeners but are living like

> **We are gardeners but are living like scarecrows. We think our job is to frighten away illinformed intruders when our job is to tend to the garden.**

scarecrows. We think our job is to frighten away ill-informed intruders when our job is to tend to the garden. We are to disciple and nurture others that have a limited understanding. You never know when one of these seemingly innocent, misguided upstarts will turn out to be a pillar in the movement and help transform thousands of lives.

When we know better, we do better. Let's help each other on both fronts. When it's time to leave the mullet behind, don't look back. Better hair is ahead.

chapter fifteen
Gathering at the Field

"I can do things you cannot,

you can do things I cannot;

together we can do great things."

—Mother Teresa

grew up in a small farming community in Kansas. While in high school, I drove a wheat truck for my best friend's dad during harvest. There are three qualifications for operating a wheat truck:

1. You have to have a pulse.
2. You have to have a driver's license.
3. You have to know how to drive a stick shift.

I had the first two covered. Not so much on number three.

Two days before the harvest began, my friend's dad took me out on a dirt road in his 1950 Chevy wheat truck (this was in the early '90s), and he taught me to drive a stick shift. When harvest came, I was ready—sort of.

With a baseball cap pulled down over the business end of my mullet, I and my 130 pounds of adolescence barely peered over the giant steering wheel as I lumbered down dusty county roads. The part of the job I dreaded most was delivering the wheat to the grain elevator. If you've ever been to the midwest, you are familiar with these enormous white structures that look like several paper towel tubes glued together. These are the skyscrapers of the great plains. At the bottom of the elevator, there is an opening where you drive in the truck. You then dump your wheat out into a steel grate on the floor. It is then lifted into the elevator where it waits to become Wheaties.

At this particular elevator, there was a significant incline leading up to the opening. This incline was no problem for me and my budding stick-shift skills as long as there was no one there ahead of me. I could barrel through the parking lot and drive the truck up in there like I owned the place. But if there was someone already there, a little piece of my soul would wither into dust. You see, if someone was in front of me, that meant that I had to park on the incline to wait, and inevitably, someone would come in behind me. I would then struggle to get this giant antique in gear and ease off the clutch without backing into the truck behind me. It was terrifying. After lurching and stalling the truck out several times on the incline, the guys working at the elevator caught on. They would see mullet boy coming and grab a railroad tie they kept off to the side. They'd place it behind my back tires, to keep me from causing an accident, and all was good in the world.

I never got completely comfortable driving the truck. I always had a sense during harvest that I was carrying a significant portion of someone else's livelihood in the back of an old truck I barely knew how to drive. For any farming community, the harvest is essential. To maximize returns on your crop, you need to be ready to start when the wheat is ripe. Once you begin, bad weather may roll in at any time and damage the crop and reduce what can be harvested. There's no time to stroll into town for lunch during harvest. Lunch is brought out to the field. You eat, and you get back to work again. Each day you cut and haul the wheat as long as daylight will allow. You can't afford a break in the action until the entire crop is in.

That's why one particular day stands out to me more than any other. I got to the field and my friend's dad let me know we'd be leaving and going over to someone else's field that day. When we arrived, we were not alone. I don't know how many wheat farmers lived in our community, but I'm sure most of them had shown up that day with their combines, wheat trucks, and hired help. I learned that the owner of this field was seriously ill and would not be able to harvest his wheat. A community member was down, and everyone stopped work in their own fields to go take care of his.

Several combines roared to life and set off into the field. One after the other, staggered like stair steps and moving in unison around the edges, they slowly worked their way through the sea of golden wheat stalks. Some of the farmers had new fancy equipment, and others had, well, 1950 Chevy wheat trucks. That day, it didn't matter. Everyone was needed. What would have normally taken many days was finished in one. Those not cutting or hauling prepared a feast to be eaten as a community among the wheat stubble at the edge of the field. As a teenager who could barely see over the steering wheel, I was undoubtedly the least qualified person in the field that day, but even I had a role to play. That day made a big impression on me. It showed me what a community working together can accomplish.

It's a beautiful picture of what foster care movement can look like in each of our communities. You show up and contribute what you have to offer. It may be a brand-new fancy laser-guided combine. It may be a beat-up old truck. You do it because, without you, everyone else carries a heavier burden, and the celebration at the end loses its richness.

If you are content with *not enough* for children and families in foster care in your community, be sure to stay in your own field. Turn newbies away when they show up. And when good things happen, take the credit.

But if you believe that *more than enough* is possible where you live, and is the only acceptable reality when it comes to children and families in foster care, then come on.

Meet us at the field.

appendix A
Your First
Four Steps

"You don't have to see the whole staircase, just take the first step."

—Dr. Martin Luther King Jr.

A chieving *more than enough* for children and families before, during, and beyond foster care in your county may feel overwhelming. It should. It is a giant God-worthy goal. As someone recently reminded me, if a turtle is on a fence post, we immediately ask who put him there. No one even considers that he might have gotten there by himself. The same is true here. When *more than enough* happens in your county, there will be no question that you didn't get there by yourself. The One who loves the brokenhearted and fights for the vulnerable will have played a most essential role in getting you there.

You don't have to have the whole thing figured out. While there may be a lot of ideas swimming around in your head, there are four critical first steps:

1. Discover your ensemble cast.
2. Put a prayer strategy in place.
3. Find out where you are.
4. Rally the troops.

1. Discover your ensemble cast.

Let's start with the easy stuff. Brainstorm every person, organization, agency, and church you know that has any involvement in foster care. This could include foster families, case workers, CASA volunteers, mentoring organizations, family law attorneys, teachers, and youth pastors. See if you can come up with at least thirty participants. This goes faster if you do it with a friend or two.

1	16
2	17
3	18
4	19
5	20
6	21
7	22
8	23
9	24
10	25
11	26
12	27
13	28
14	29
15	30

You will create a master contact list from this group (a Google sheet is a great way to do this and will facilitate future collaboration). Provide columns to track your interactions, their interest in collaborating, and basic info about the things they are involved in.

2. Put a prayer strategy in place.

A good place to start is to identify those in your community who might already be praying together on a regular basis and find out if it is possible to introduce the subject of children in foster care as a part of their normal prayer times.

Beyond that, here are a few other ways that you can make prayer a foundational part of your movement-building effort early on:

- Gather for an evening with others in your community for a foster care prayer vigil. While you can do this at any time of the year, Focus on the Family sponsors the National Foster Care Prayer Vigil in May each year (visit FosterCarePrayerVigil.org).
- Start a local, weekly fifteen-minute foster care prayer call (early mornings or lunchtimes work great). We suggest using a video conference service like Zoom. We've found that people are more likely to keep coming when there is face-to-face interaction on a video call.
- Join an existing, weekly fifteen-minute state foster care prayer call by visiting MoreThanEnoughTogether.org.

(To help facilitate your prayer times, you can find our National Foster Care Prayer Guide at https://resources. cafo.org/resource/foster-care-prayer-guide/)

3. Find out where you are.

You should begin by finding out some basic information. As we discussed in Chapter 8, building relationships with key people in your local child welfare office or a private agency may be necessary to uncover this data. You may not be able to find every piece of information listed here, but the more you can find the better foundation you will have going forward.

	In My County	In My State
# of Children in Care		
# of Licensed Foster Families		
# of Children Placed out of County		
# of Children in Care with Adoption as Their Case Plan Goal		
# of Biological Family Units Represented by the Children in Care		
# of Churches*		

*To determine the number of churches where you live, refer to our free PDF guide, "Church Numbers by County" at https://MoreThanEnoughTogether.org/resources/

As you interact with child welfare professionals and agencies, keep these questions in mind. They will help you get a more complete picture of the current state of affairs:

- In your opinion, what are the most significant challenges facing vulnerable families in our community?
- What do you think could be done to help these families so fewer children end up in foster care?
- What challenges have you encountered in recruiting foster and adoptive families?
- Once a potential adoptive or foster family comes to an informational meeting, what barriers do you see that might prevent them from completing the process?
- What new initiatives or ideas are you working on that you are most excited about?
- What areas of the foster care system would you most like to see change?
- What organizations, leaders, or councils do you currently work with to coordinate efforts for community involvement?
- Have you ever partnered with churches on the issue of foster care in the past? If so, how did it work? What were the challenges? What went well?
- I am interested in learning as much as possible about how churches in our community can best serve kids and families in foster care. Who else should I be talking to?
- Is there anything else you feel is important for me to know as I explore?[56]

4. Rally the Troops

Once you've found your core ensemble cast, built a simple prayer strategy, and gathered some initial data about the current situation, it is time to get a larger group together in the same room. Your goal here is to gather key people together to cast vision and explore the possibilities. Your ongoing strategic planning will be conducted by a much smaller team (your ensemble cast) on a once or twice per month basis. However, this event is a way of gathering a more significant number of key leaders in your community around this issue. Here are a few tips from those who have done these kinds of events before:

Host the event collaboratively.

It should be hosted collaboratively by a group of churches rather than by a government agency, a private agency, or even a single church. How you set this gathering up sends an essential message to the county and state and to other churches in the community. If the state or a private agency hosts the gathering, churches will see it as another program they are being asked to send their people to and they won't feel a sense of responsibility and ownership for the outcome. If a single church hosts it, the state may feel uneasy about being publicly associated with one particular church/ denomination. However, when a group of churches hosts together, it sends the right message to everyone. Churches recognize their role in helping to lead the community in this area, private agencies can fill the role of serving the churches well, and the state is put in the favorable position of partnering with a broad group of representatives from the faith community. Win-win-win.

Host it at a church.

While a whole group of churches should host the event, it is usually a good idea for one of those churches to provide the meeting space for the event. Again, this sends a message to everyone involved that churches are taking responsibility to help address the foster care crisis in that community. This is not a government or agency program for churches to jump on board with.

Start on the right foot.

While this may be the first event of its type in your community, remember that there is a lot of history involved, and it would be wise to humbly acknowledge that. When you select those who will be facilitating and speaking, it's incredibly important that the messages involve the following: (1) positive encouragement and gratitude toward the county and state (no matter how many things you may feel are wrong with the system); (2) an acknowledgment and even an apology from a pastor toward the state, admitting that the church has not been as involved in these issues as it should have been and committing that you are all there that day to humbly ask what you can do to help; (3) a humble position of service and partnership (rather than a rallying cry that says, "The church is here to take over and fix things!").

Get the people involved.

We suggest setting up the room with tables rather than rows of chairs. The whole point of this meeting is collaboration, not merely listening to inspiring speakers. You'll want to mix things up, so that church representatives and county/state representatives are sitting together throughout the room. Make sure there is plenty of time in the schedule for table discussion and brainstorming related to identifying the following: (1) things that are working well, (2) obstacles to achieving *more than enough*, and (3) ideas for moving forward.

Feed them well.

This kind of event is *perfect* for asking a local restaurant to provide a meal or dessert at a discount or even for free. It is a community gathering designed to creatively and collaboratively address the needs of foster care. Make sure everyone at the event knows who provided the food.[57]

These first four steps can be completed in a matter of months. After that, it will be all about continuing to meet regularly (no less than once a month) with your ensemble cast (we recommend six to eight leaders and probably no more than twelve). You will use what you learn from these first four steps to agree on the problem you are going to address and then will build a strategic plan from there. Your ensemble cast will likely include someone with experience in the facilitation of a strategic planning process. A lot could be said about strategic planning, but here's one key: start small and simple. Don't feel you need to do everything at once. Certainly, we should work to build a broad understanding of the foster system and the challenges facing children and families in the community. But first choosing to focus on a few, or even just one, specific priority is key to your success. Overextension leads to shoddy programs and exhausted people. But narrow focus produces good results that build both trust and positive momentum.

Stay committed to meeting, building trust, resolving conflict, and fighting together for kids and families in your community until there is *more than enough.*

Credit Report

As the pages of this book have detailed, it takes a lot of people to do big things. In most books, this section would be called the acknowledgments. However, a "credit report" seemed more appropriate in this case (see chapter 13).

To my amazing bride, Trisha — when we moved into a downtown neighborhood to love kids and families 23 years ago, we had no idea what domino we were landing on. One thing led to another, we eventually signed up for foster parent training classes, and brought home some sick babies. Now we have a crazy life we both never could have imagined and always dreamed of. Babe, it is your Kingdom thinking that is all over these pages. I'm so glad I'm doing this with you.

To my kids, Cecilia, Carmen, Moriah, Joshua, and Sophia — you are amazing. You all are fighters and remind me every day why I do what I do. I believe we can use our words to change things, and I pray that you will grow up believing that too.

To my big brother, Todd Weber — thank you for your insight on bass fishing tournaments that helped me sound a little more like I knew what I was talking about. Thank you also for showing my kids how to hold a fish way out in front of them to make it look bigger in photographs (um, was I supposed to keep that a secret?).

As a part of the Christian Alliance for Orphans (CAFO) team, I have the privilege of working with a group of incredibly generous, spiritually grounded, and intelligent world-changers. Amanda Baird, you have really outdone yourself on this one. Thank you for keeping this project on track and for your wise insight on *so many things*. Thanks for listening to me think out loud and for murmuring "uh huh" at appropriate intervals. Also, the section in the book about the Muppets would not be the same without you. Karl Dinkler, working remotely as a team is most challenging when it comes to kicking around creative ideas. If we were actually in the same building together, I'd just move a lawn chair in your office so that we could sit and figure out everything together. I love being able to give you a call when I'm stuck. David Hennessey, you are a movement-builder through and through with the heart of Nehemiah. Jason Johnson, it's a privilege to be mistaken for you from time to time. Thank you for your commitment to excellence and the thoughtfulness with which you approach everything you do. Jedd Medefind, your servant leadership is inspiring. Thank you for your passion for the *More Than Enough* vision, your constant encouragement, for how you beautifully model going deep first, and for all of your tremendous help with the text found on these pages. Ashley Phelan, you have played such a critical role in the collaborative development of the *More Than Enough* vision. Thank you for always cheerfully jumping into whatever needed to be done to move the ball down the field. Ashley Reyes, I am grateful for your joy-filled willingness to make things more beautiful and more impactful for the sake of kids and families. You do so much to keep the machinery of CAFO running. Brandie Smith, you are such an encourager and a prayer warrior. You provide the structures to help all of us turn our passions and dreams into real things (like this book) that help children and families. Elizabeth Wiebe, thank you for always creating such amazing spaces for ideas to be shared and relationships to be built between all the members of the CAFO community. So much of the collaborative work being done around the country that is described in this book was bolstered by your efforts. Nicole Wilke, I am so grateful for your ability to take heady ideas and turn them into practical things that anyone can use to create change in their communities. Your insights on how to help the rest of us use data for life change are invaluable. And to the rest of CAFO team, thank you for continually teaching me what "better together" looks like. I am so grateful for you.

I want to thank an extraordinary group of friends who are deeply passionate about the *More Than Enough* vision, have been instrumental in shaping it, and have sacrificed a great deal of time, energy, and resources for the good of organizations, advocates, children and families way beyond the scope of their own individual work: Drake Bassett, Andy Cook, Dr. Sharen Ford, Adrien Lewis, Brian Mavis, Scott Platter, Shelly Radic, and Janet Rowland. It's been one of my greatest joys to work with each of you. Thank you.

One of my highest priorities in writing this book was that it reflect the best practices and best thinking out there about the subjects that it touches. For that to happen, many people influenced the ideas in this book both directly by providing feedback on specific chapters in their areas of expertise and indirectly by modeling the philosophies and practices at the heart of the *More Than Enough* movement. It's a long list of some of the best people I know (you get bonus points if you can read all the names without taking a breath): Bishop Aaron Blake, Melissa Blum, Bob Bruder-Mattson, Whitney Bunker, Chris Campbell, Jane Chaffee, Lauri Currier, Michelle Douglas, Kerri Dunkleberger, Christie Erwin, Kevin Enders, Gabe Forsyth, Diego Fuller, Chelsea Geyer, Riley Green, Dr. Jerry Haag, Ashley Haeusler, Janet Kelly, Bruce and Denise Kendrick, Rhonda Littleton, Tom Lukasik, Samela Macon, Rod Marshall, Laura Mobley, Johnston Moore, Herbie Newell, Katie O'Dell, Jenni Olowo, Chris Palusky, Philip Pattison, Lesli Reece, Christie Mac Segars, Kondo Simkufwe, Ryan Stanton, Toni Steere, Cecil Stokes, Nicole Taylor, Trent Taylor, Donald Verleur, David and Cara Von Tress, Darren Washausen, and Maddi Wycoff.

Thank you to Tim Beals at Credo Publishing, who has demonstrated such kindness and flexibility. Thank you to editor, Elizabeth Banks, who has played such an essential role in adding clarity to the text. Thank you to graphic designer, Frank Gutbrod, who has elegantly rendered the ideas of this book and brought such clarity and beauty. Lori Bailey, thank you for the fantastic illustrations that add such a beautiful dimension to the ideas in this book.

To each person here, thank you. We are better together.

Endnotes

1   Martine Berg Olsen, "Fly single-handedly ruined domino world record attempt," *Metro.co.uk*, 5 August 2018, metro.co.uk/2018/08/05/fly-single-handedly-ruined-domino-world-record-attempt-7799849/.

2   Karen Strike, "The Paint by Numbers Phenomenon Made Dan Robbins the Most Exhibited Artist in the World," *Flashbak.com*, 2 November 2018, flashbak.com/paint-by-numbers-dan-robbins-art-407356/.

3   Jason Daley, "Thank Dan Robbins for the Paint-by-Number Craze," *Smithsonian Magazine*, 8 April 2019, www.smithsonianmag.com/smart-news/dan-robbins-who-launched-paint-number-craze-1950s-has-died-180971888/.

4   *Finding Nemo.* Directed by Andrew Stanton, Walt Disney Pictures. 30 May 2003.

5   J. E. Hansan, "Charles Loring Brace," Virginia Commonwealth University Social Welfare History Project, 2011, http://www.socialwelfarehistory.com/people/brace-charles-loring/.

6   "History of Foster Care in the United States," National Foster Parent Association, accessed 4 October 2019, nfpaonline.org/page-1105741.

7   "History" Children's Bureau, An Office of the Administration for Children and Families, accessed 4 October 2019, www.acf.hhs.gov/cb/about/history.

8   "United States Code: Social Security Act, 42 U.S.C. §§ 301–1305 Suppl. 4 1934." Library of Congress, accessed 4 October 2019, www.loc.gov/item/uscode1934-005042007/.

9   Jason Johnson, *Everyone Can Do Something.* (Grand Rapids: Credo House Publishers, 2018).

10   John Kelly, Daniel Heimpel, Jeremy Loudenback, Christie Renick, Kim Phagan-Hansel, Elizabeth Green, Stephanie Pham, and Marisol Zarate, "The Foster Care Housing Crisis," The Chronicle of Social Change, accessed 23 August 2019, chronicleofsocialchange.org/wp-content/uploads/2017/10/The-Foster-Care-Housing-Crisis-10-31.pdf.

11   "Children in child welfare system who have been adopted by pre-adoptive relationship with adoptive parents in the United States" October 2019, Annie E. Casey Foundation, Kids Count Data Center, datacenter.kidscount.org/data/tables/6678-children-in-child-welfare-system-who-have-been-adopted-by-pre-adoptive-relationship-with-adoptive-parents?loc=1&loct=2#detailed/2/2-53/true/870,573,869,36,868,867,133,38,35,18/2978,2977,2976,2975/13732,13733.

12   John Kelly, "Who Cares: A National Count of Foster Homes and Families," Chronicle of Social Change, 15 October 2018, chronicleofsocialchange.org/child-welfare-2/cares-national-count-foster-homes-families/32481.

13   "Adoption Stats for Kids in Foster Care Get Updated," Annie E. Casey Foundation, Kids Count Data Center, 17 September 2018, datacenter.kidscount.org/updates/show/212-adoption-stats-for-kids-in-foster-care.

14 "Children in foster care waiting for adoption by amount of time waiting in the United States" Annie E. Casey Foundation, Kids Count Data Center, October 2019, datacenter.kidscount. org/data/tables/6679-children-in-foster-care-waiting-for-adoption-by-amount-of-time-waiting#detailed/1/any/false/870,573,869,36,868,867,133,38,35,18/2980,2983,2982,2984,2981,2986/13735,13734.

15 "Fact Sheets: Foster Care" Children's Rights, accessed 23 August 2019, www.childrensrights.org/newsroom/fact-sheets/foster-care/.

16 *Chariots of Fire*. Directed by Hugh Hudson, Allied Stars Ltd, Goldcrest Films, Enigma Productions and The Ladd Company, 9 April 1982.

17 "The Afcars Report," U.S. Dept. of Health and Human Services, Administration for Children and Families, Administration on Children, Youth and Families, Children's Bureau, 10 August 2018, www.acf.hhs.gov/sites/default/files/cb/afcarsreport25.pdf.

18 "Foster Care Statistics 2017," Child Welfare Information Gateway, U.S. Department of Health and Human Services, Children's Bureau, March 2019, www.childwelfare.gov/pubPDFs/foster.pdf.

19 "Stats Show Our Nation's Foster Care System Is in Trouble," National Council for Adoption, 4 January 2008, www.adoptioncouncil.org/blog/2018/01/stats-show-our-nations-foster-care-system-is-in-trouble.

20 Jenn Rexroad, "Why Keeping Current Foster Parents Can Be More Important Than Recruiting New Ones," The Chronicle of Social Change, 28 November 2018, chronicleofsocialchange.org/child-welfare-2/why-keeping-foster-parents-is-just-as-important-as-recruiting-new-ones/32849.

21   Jia Wertz, "Don't Spend 5 Times More Attracting New Customers, Nurture the Existing Ones," Forbes, 12 September 2018,   www.forbes.com/sites/jiawertz/2018/09/12/dont-spend-5-times-more-attracting-new-customers-nurture-the-existing-ones/#527c08055a8e.

22   T. Reilly and L. Platz, "Post-Adoption Service Needs of Families with Special Needs Children: Use, Helpfulness, and Unmet Needs," *Journal of Social Service Research*, 30, no. 4 (2004), 51–67. doi.org/10.1300/J079v30n04_03

23   Chip Heath and Dan Heath. Switch: *How to Change Things When Change Is Hard*. New York, Random House, 2010.

24   Peter Greer and Chris Horst with Jill Heisey, *Rooting for Rivals: How Collaboration and Generosity Increase the Impact of Leaders, Charities, and Churches* (Bloomington, MN: Bethany House Publishers, 2018).

25   Hugo Young, Bryan Silcock, Peter M. Dunn, *Journey to Tranquility* (London: Jonathon Cape, 1969).

26   Chip Heath and Dan Heath, *Decisive: How to Make Better Choices in Life and Work* (New York: Penguin Random House, 2013).

27   "Starting the Dialogue with Your Local Child Welfare Office" used with permission from *Church and State Partnerships*, CAFO Foster Movement, 2018.

28   Roberto A. Ferdman, "Baby Carrots Are Not Baby Carrots," 13 January 2016, The Washington Post, https://www.washingtonpost.com/news/wonk/wp/2016/01/13/no-one-understands-baby-carrots/.

29   Roberto A. Ferdman, "Baby Carrots Are Not Baby Carrots," 13 January 2016, The Washington Post, https://www.washingtonpost.com/news/wonk/wp/2016/01/13/no-one-understands-baby-carrots/.

30   Jamie Ballard, "Chocolate Is the Most Popular Ice Cream Flavor," 10 July 2018, Today.com, https://today.yougov.com/topics/food/articles-reports/2018/07/10/most-popular-ice-creams.

31   "Child Welfare Outcomes Report Data," 2013–17, Children's Bureau, An Office of the Administration for Children & Families, https://cwoutcomes.acf.hhs.gov/cwodatasite/.

32   Mike Montgomery, "What Entrepreneurs Can Learn from the Philanthropic Struggles of TOMS Shoes," 28 April 2015, Forbes.com, https://www.forbes.com/sites/mikemontgomery/2015/04/28/how-entrepreneurs-can-avoid-the-philanthropy-pitfalls/#3758299a1c38).

33   Mike Montgomery, "What Entrepreneurs Can Learn from the Philanthropic Struggles of TOMS Shoes," 28 April 2015, Forbes.com, https://www.forbes.com/sites/mikemontgomery/2015/04/28/how-entrepreneurs-can-avoid-the-philanthropy-pitfalls/#3758299a1c38).

34   John Kania and Mark Kramer, "Collective Impact," Stanford Social Innovation Review, Winter 2011, ssir.org/articles/entry/collective_impact.

35   John Kania and Mark Kramer, "Collective Impact," Stanford Social Innovation Review, Winter 2011, ssir.org/articles/entry/collective_impact.

36   John Kania and Mark Kramer, "Collective Impact," Stanford Social Innovation Review, Winter 2011, ssir.org/articles/entry/collective_impact.

37   *The Muppet Movie.* Directed by James Frawley, ITC Entertainment, Henson Associates, Associated Film Distribution, 22 June 1979.

38   Child Welfare Information Gateway, "How the Child Welfare System Works," U.S. Department of Health and Human

Services, Children's Bureau, 2013, www.childwelfare.gov/pubs/factsheets/cpswork/.

39   Jedd Medefind, "Iron Sharpens Iron," NFCI Symposium, online video clip, 20 August 2014, https://vimeo.com/nfcisymposium.

40   Chart used with permission from the Christian Alliance for Orphans. "How to Speak Up for Kids in Foster Care: A Quick Guide to Approaching Government Leaders," April 2018, https://resources.cafo.org/resource/how-to-speak-up/.

41   William Shakespeare, *Romeo and Juliet*, 1597. Oxford: published for the Malone Society by Oxford University Press, 2000.

42   SparkNotes editors. (2005) *No Fear Romeo and Juliet.* www.sparknotes.com/nofear/shakespeare/romeojuliet/.

43   *Star Wars Episode IV: A New Hope.* Directed by George Lucas, Lucasfilm Ltd., Twentieth Century Fox, 25 May 1977.

44   *Jaws.* Directed by Steven Spielberg, Zanuck/Brown Company, Universal Pictures, 20 June 1975.

45   *The Princess Bride.* Directed by Rob Reiner, Act III Communications, Buttercup Films, The Princes Bride Ltd., Twentieth Century Fox, 25 September 1987.

46   *The Shawshank Redemption.* Directed by Frank Darabont, Castle Rock Entertainment, Columbia Pictures. 10 September 1994.

47   *Back to the Future.* Directed by Robert Zemeckis, Amblin Entertainment, Universal Pictures, 3 July 1985.

48   *The Lion King.* Directed by Robert Minkoff and Roger Allers, Walt Disney Pictures. 15 June 1994.

49   *The Wizard of Oz.* Directed by Victor Fleming, Metro-Goldwyn-Mayer, Loew's Inc. 25 August 1953.

50   "Jason Witten's Full Retirement Press Conference," 3 May

2018, National Football League, www.nfl.com/videos/up-to-the-minute/oap3000000931406/Jason-Witten-s-full-retirement-press-conference.

51 Paul J. Zak, "The Neuroscience of Trust," Harvard Business Review, January–February 2017, hbr.org/2017/01/the-neuroscience-of-trust.

52 "Encourage" *Lexico.com*. Oxford University Press (OUP). 2019. https://www.lexico.com/en/definition/encourage.

53 Randy Conley, "4 Ways to Overcome the Danger of False Humility," Leading with Trust, 6 October 2019, leadingwithtrust.com/2019/10/06/4-ways-to-overcome-the-danger-of-false-humility/#comments.

54 "Some Breakfast Cereals Marketed to Kids Are More Than 50 Percent Sugar," Consumer Reports, 1 October 2008, https://valenciacollege.edu/students/library/mla-apa-chicago-guides/documents/Consumer-Reports-MLA.pdf.

55 Jessica Dweck, "Whence the Mullet? The History of Iran's Forbidden Haircut," Slate, 10 July 2010, https://slate.com/news-and-politics/2010/07/the-history-of-the-mullet-iran-s-forbidden-haircut.html.

56 Adapted from "Church and State Partnerships in Foster Care: Six Places Where It's Working." by CAFO Foster Movement. https://resources.cafo.org/resource/church-state-partners-foster-care-6-places-working/

57 Adapted from "Growing a Foster Care Movement in Your Community" by CAFO Foster Movement. https://resources.cafo.org/resource/grow-foster-movement/

About the Author

Jason Weber and his wife, Trisha, have been speaking up on behalf of the marginalized for the past 24 years. As licensed foster parents for over a decade, they had the privilege of adopting their five kids from foster care. Jason has written and helped to produce several books and other tools, including *Farmer Herman and the Flooding Barn*, a 2018 ECPA Christian Book Award finalist. Jason writes a regular column for *Fostering Families Today* magazine and is the host of the *Foster Movement Podcast*, which highlights the stories of former foster youth and national foster care advocates. Jason serves with the Christian Alliance for Orphans (CAFO) and helps lead *More Than Enough*, a collaborative movement facilitated by the CAFO community. Jason and his family live in Plano, Texas.

Christian Alliance for Orphans

The Christian Alliance for Orphans is a coordinated alliance of 200+ organizations, along with more than 700 churches and countless individuals and families — all working together in shared initiatives to grow innovative solutions and effective care for vulnerable children and families. To learn more, visit *CAFO.org*.

EVERYONE CAN DO SOMETHING

*A Field-Guide for Strategically Rallying Your Church
Around the Orphaned and Vulnerable*

Whether you are launching a new foster care, adoption
or orphan care ministry or leading an existing one, you'll
discover the principles you need to take the next best steps
for your church, your ministry and the families and children
you are serving.

everyonecandosomethingbook.com

More Than Enough is possible in your county.

And *you* play a vital role.

Visit the ***More Than Enough*** website to:

- Discover additional resources that can help you in your county

- Take the **FREE** 10-minute ***More Than Enough*** Church Assessment and get a customized report

- Sign the ***More Than Enough*** Declaration

MoreThanEnoughTogether.org